Tracy Tennant and her writing opens the eyes of those who are searching for truth. Her books are a huge help to doubting and former Mormons who want to know the real Jesus and have a genuine relationship with him outside the misconception of a life devoted to a church and having faith in leaders rather than in Christ alone. Tracy's walk and expressions of love in her books reach out to those in need of finding a Jesus whose love is unconditional and who gives light to those searching for him. Her stories and teaching helps you find and put Jesus Christ first and in the center of your heart and soul. Thank you Tracy for sharing your love for ex-Mormons in this book and for the love you put into writing it. Thank you for expressing your love for our Savior and helping those who are searching for Him.

Louie D. ~ Former Mormon

I just finished your book. Thank you! It was such a blessing to me. I believe it will help so many ex-Mormons in their recovery from Mormonism. I could relate to everything you wrote about. I wish I could have read it when I first realized the church was false. It would have kept me from making many of the mistakes you warned about. Your advice and suggestions will help ex-Mormons heal and avoid additional heartache. It is so comforting to know that we are not alone, and that there is a light at the end of the tunnel. God bless you and your ministry.

Amy C.~ Former Mormon

I really enjoyed this book and am so glad you took the time to write down your experiences and thoughts for others to share in and not feel so alone. It was very informative and an uplifting read for those struggling with, or in the process of, leaving Mormonism and dealing with all that entails.

Becky W. ~ Former Mormon

CONFESSIONS OF AN EX-MORMON

From Kolob to Calvary
Volume 1

CONFESSIONS OF AN EX-MORMON

WHAT I WISH I KNEW WHEN I LEFT THE CHURCH

Tracy Tennant

Olathe, Kansas

The contents of this book are the opinions and experiences of the author and should not be regarded as a substitute for professional counseling, therapy, or legal advice. Important decisions affecting your life and the lives of your loved ones should be made after consulting with a member of the clergy, professional counselor, therapist, or lawyer. Individuals leaving Mormonism have their own unique circumstances, which are complex and often difficult. Only you know your situation best. The author and publisher shall not be liable for any problems alledgedly arising from using suggestions or information in this book.

Right Track Publishing, P.O. Box 4712, Olathe, KS 66063
righttrackpublishing.com
From Kolob to Calvary Series, Volume 1
First Edition (eBook): April 2014
First Print Edition: March 2017
Printed in the United States of America
ISBN: 978-0-9913371-1-8
Library of Congress Control Number: 2017934547

RELIGION / Christianity / Church of Jesus Christ of Latter-day Saints (Mormon)
RELIGION / Christian Life / Relationships
SELF HELP / Spirituality

Dedicated to those who leave Mormonism and still believe Jesus is the way, the truth, and the life. May you find healing in His arms.

CONTENTS

Introduction

The series *From Kolob to Calvary* is for people who have left or are in the process of leaving Mormonism, but still believe Jesus is the way, the truth, and the life. Whatever your reasons for leaving the Church of Jesus Christ of Latter-day Saints—aka Mormon Church or LDS Church—you've come to the conclusion that it isn't what it claims to be: "the only true and living church upon the face of the whole earth" (Doctrine & Covenants 1:30). Now what? You might be asking yourself some of the following questions:

- How will my spouse or children react?
- Will my spouse leave me?
- What will my LDS relatives say?
- How should I respond to ward members?
- Should I have my name removed from the record?
- Will I lose my job with my LDS employer?
- Will I get kicked out of my LDS school?
- Can the Bible or Christianity be trusted?
- What church should I join, if any?

Leaving the Church is a complex issue with too many variables and dynamics to cover in-depth in a small series of books. Each situation has its own set of special needs; however, there are basic principles that apply regardless of your circumstances. If you need individualized advice or counseling for your specific circumstance, please consider speaking to a pastor who has experience with former Mormons and is knowledgeable about Mormonism, or get a referral for a Christian counselor or lawyer.

This book is intended to assist you in your transition out of Mormonism by giving you a few tools and guidelines to make it as painless as possible and help you once again to feel that you have hope and purpose.

At this point you've made or are in process of making the difficult decision to leave the Church. You're exhausted from reading, researching, staying up late, and losing sleep. On the one hand, you're tired of being told what to do. On the other hand, it would be a relief if someone would tell you what to do. You're bouncing back and forth like a pinball between an array of emotions; and to top things off—if you haven't experienced it yet—there's going to be fallout; collateral damage associated with your decision to separate yourself from Mormonism.

Following is an example of what you might be going through, excerpted from an article I wrote, *The Proper Care and Feeding of Ex-Mormons*; and from my book, *Mormonism, the Matrix, and Me*;

> Imagine going home to your parents' house to visit. You go to the attic to look for something, and while poking around you find a small chest with some papers in it. You examine the documents and learn, to your horror, that you were born the opposite sex. So, if you are now a man you learn you were born female, and if you are a woman you learn you were born male. You were born the opposite of what your parents wanted, so they arranged for a sex-change operation when you were still an infant. Everything that you had thought about yourself, others, and the world was built on a lie. All the time you were growing up you felt different and

didn't know why. The way you looked at life was based on who you thought you were and what you believed was true.

If something like this happened, your world would crumble around you. You wouldn't know what to trust, let alone who to trust. You would have to re-learn almost everything; the way you interacted with others, the way you dressed, and so much more, assuming you decided to return to the gender you were born as. Even if you stayed the artificial gender there would be psychological ramifications. What if you had married? What if every major decision you made was based on what you thought was truth—that you were a man (or a woman)? There would be so much fallout your head would be spinning. You would most likely experience rage, despair, grief, sorrow, anguish, mistrust, and confusion.

This is the closest analogy I can think of to describe what people coming out of Mormonism go through. The longer they were members of the Church and the more they genuinely believed it to be true, the more severe their distress coming out. Someone who had been LDS all his or her life experiences greater tumult than someone who was a convert of only a year or two. However, even those who leave the Church after just a couple years experience a great sense of loss.

Obviously, the analogy only goes so far. In the story the parents foisted the deception knowingly upon the child. In real life, members of the Church are not intentionally deceiving people. This analogy is meant only to illustrate the emotional devastation many Mormons experience when they believe they've been played for fools. I, for one, certainly felt several of the emotions described in the story; at first disbelief, followed by anger, then sorrow, loss, and a sense of purposelessness, depression, and finally—after a few years—healing.

The good news is that healing is possible; sometimes partial, sometimes full. It just takes time, patience, and forgiveness of self and others. Some scars might never go away, as in cases where a TBM (True Blue Mormon, True Believing Mormon) spouse divorces you or tries to keep you from your children. You might feel alone and wonder if anyone else is going through the same heartache as you. The answer is a resounding yes! A surprising (or maybe unsurprising) number of people are exiting the Mormon Church every day; enough to cause concern among LDS Church officials. Look at the increasing number of General Conference talks that address the issue of so-called apostasy or the number of ex-Mormon recovery groups on social media and in larger communities all over the world (U.S. in particular).

Family devastation, broken relationships, and ostracism resulting from leaving the Church, however, is not exclusive to Mormonism. Whenever there are deeply-held beliefs and religious convictions within families or communities—whether Mormon, Muslim, Jewish, Catholic, Fundamentalist, Protestant, or what-have-you—personal conflicts are inevitable when individuals leave that circle of faith.

The presumption in this series is that you still have faith in God and embrace a Judeo-Christian worldview. As you go through the process of leaving Mormonism behind and preserving or reconciling your relationships, remember to rely on God's strength. Be prayerful. Be careful. And don't beat yourself up when you blow it. We all make mistakes. Countless ex-Mormons have made mistakes. We've said and done things we wish we hadn't. That's part of being human. That's what this book in the series *From Kolob to Calvary* is about: the mistakes I and others have made as we left Mormonism and the things we could have done differently. I hope it will be helpful in your exodus.

That being said, it's time to get started with moving ahead, establishing peace with those you love most, and regaining your sense of purpose and mission.

1

What to Expect From LDS Family and Friends

"Trials teach us what we are; they dig up the soil, and let us see what we are made of."
~ Charles Spurgeon

I ran a survey for ex-LDS Christians to complete. The dozens of responses were bittersweet and poignant; but full of encouragement and hope as well. I'll share some of their answers, and throughout the book include my own experiences in leaving the Church after 26 years as a "True Blue Mormon."

Question: What was the biggest challenge you faced after discovering Mormonism wasn't true?

Telling my husband that I was leaving the Church.

Explaining to my kids that I had led them into a cult.

Letting go of some of the doctrines that influenced my daily life. Understanding that it wasn't my parents' fault, and even the fault of most of my church leaders for teaching me that the Church was true. Understanding that they were deceived just like me.

Being rejected and even shunned by most of my Mormon family.

Facing family members in Utah and being shunned and bullied by most of them. However, a lot of my family has now left the Church too.

Knowing where to go from there. I wanted God, but I'd never been to a church other than the LDS church before. I was too scared to go by myself.

The respondents' answers reflect what the majority of former members face as they leave the Church. They are often avoided, rejected, and shunned by family and ward members. Whether or not leaders encourage such treatment by members of those who leave the Church is a moot point. It happens, and we are left to deal with the consequences. LDS leaders might argue that the Church teaches only love and kindness, but the reality is that former-Mormons suffer because of the words and actions of their active, believing counterparts.

In my 16+ years of ministry helping individuals as they transition out of Mormonism, I've witnessed heartbreaking accounts of rejection and betrayal. One just has to shake his head in sorrow and disbelief that people can be so intentionally hurtful to someone just because they believe differently. Be that as it may, as some ex-LDS have kept in contact with me over months or years, I've seen good things—even great things—result in their lives, although it was a long road getting there. There was light at the end of the tunnel (no, not an oncoming train) and they moved on to healing and greater happiness.

In this chapter, I'll cover three groups from whom you can expect reactions: ward members and friends, extended family, and immediate family (which can be parents if you live at home or a spouse and children if you're married). Special circumstances, like dating or being engaged to an active Mormon, also fall into the category of immediate family. Later we'll explore different ways to announce your decision, make your exit, and possible ways to handle reactions.

Ward Members and Friends

Once you announce your decision to stop attending the ward, several things will happen. Ward members divide into three different camps: those who try to convince you to come back, those who pretend nothing has happened, and those who become angry and actually shun you. You can expect the bishop, home teachers, and visiting teachers to reach out to you through visits and phone calls. Members who were in your circle of friends or were close to you through your church calling will most likely want to know why you are leaving or have left. You might be "love bombed" with cards or plates of cookies, phone calls, and people asking if you were offended in some way.

LDS friends outside the ward will want to know what's going on. They may invite you to lunch to talk about it. They might try to argue with you to convince you that the books or articles you've read or the websites you've visited are nothing but "anti-Mormon spiritual porn." They might tell you that you were a "valiant and chosen spirit" in the preexistence, and that Satan is doing everything he can to lead you astray.

If you try to maintain relationships with ward members—either because you don't want to lose those connections or because you still have family members attending the ward—you can expect mixed reactions that bring awkwardness to social situations.

Here are a couple of examples. A few months after I left the Church (my husband and teens were still attending), I had the opportunity to get day-old bakery items and produce from a friend who was part of a food outreach to the poor. Whatever she had left after distributing the grocery items to various organizations she gave to me to do with as I wished. Since I had been the Relief Society president, I was aware of about seven families in the ward who were really struggling financially. So, for a couple months I picked up the extra groceries from my friend, sorted them into bags, and delivered them to these families along with handwritten notes of encouragement. I wasn't doing this out of any ulterior motive. I did this because I knew there was a need and I wanted to show ward members that I hadn't stopped caring about them even though I no longer participated in the ward. The reactions I got were interesting.

One of the women seemed truly grateful. She and her husband were fairly new members of the Church and hadn't been in our ward for long. Through my visiting teaching I knew that her husband had a serious gambling problem (this was in Las Vegas), and she was depressed and discouraged. When I came with bags of groceries, she let me in her house and we would talk for a few minutes. She always thanked me and seemed truly appreciative.

There were a couple places where I knew the family was home. I could see cars in the driveway and movement of the curtains, but no one would open the door. I just left the food on the porch and then smiled and waved toward the window before driving away.

I suppose the most hurtful reaction was from a divorced woman with children whom I had visit-taught for a couple years. One of her daughters was close friends with my daughter. Every time I brought the groceries, the woman would open the door only a crack, and then hesitantly open it enough to squeeze through, close the door behind her, and stand on the porch eyeing me suspiciously. I tried to engage her in conversation, but her answers were short. I would tell her I hoped she was having a good week, and then leave. Her behavior led me to wonder if she really used the food for her family or if she threw it all away out of fear that eating it would cause "apostasy seeds" to sprout in their digestive tracts and make them leave the Church too.

My stint as a Grocery Angel only lasted a couple of months before my friend was no longer in the food drive program, but the experience opened my eyes to the strong feelings evoked in others by my departure from the Church.

Another experience was at a ward party held at a prominent member's home. The man was a politician of some sort (city councilman or assemblyman), and every year he and his wife held a big shindig for ward members. Their home sat on a couple acres, and they had small farm equipment, chickens, goats, and calves. They hosted a big barbecue, with lots of food and fun activities for kids. My kids didn't want to miss out, so I went with them (dressed in a tank top and mid-thigh length shorts) (shame on me, I know).

Some ward members ignored me until I made efforts to converse with them. They politely, albeit awkwardly, chatted for a few minutes before moving on. Other people outright avoided me. When they saw me heading in their direction, they walked away. There were a few—the bishop and my Relief Society counselors—who went out of their way to greet me, ask me how I was doing, and make me feel like I wasn't a complete pariah.

For the first six or seven years after I left the Church, I sent Christmas cards to about 25 families in the ward. I always included a short letter about how our family was doing, a brief praise report on the ways God had blessed us that year, and expressed my wishes for them to have a new year full of rich blessings. I always felt bad that I never heard back from them, except for a few cards stamped "Return to Sender." The funny part (at least it's funny to me) is that the only person I always got a Christmas card from was the guy in the ward who was the politician. I can only assume he cared more about securing my vote than he did about making me feel like a real person as an ex-Mormon.

You'll probably find your experiences to be similar to mine if you try to maintain relationships with people in the ward. Emotions run wide and deep on both sides when someone leaves the Church, especially if it was abrupt and conspicuous. There's a big difference between a relatively inactive member slipping quietly out of view and someone with a high-profile calling going AWOL. When a high-profile Church member suddenly announces they no longer have a testimony, and in fact, has come across evidence that the Church isn't true, it then becomes a matter of damage control. Leaders try to keep ward members from asking too many questions. Parents speculate or make up reasons for the person's departure so as to ensure the testimonies of their own teenagers aren't shaken.

When a cult can no longer control you, it will try to control how others see you.

You can expect your reputation to become M.U.D. (Mormon Untrue Defamation). I was serving as Relief Society President when I defected. A few months later my husband also left. He was one of the High Priest Group teachers. After we both left the Church, all kinds of rumors began flying. One rumor was that we were "swingers" (swapping marriage partners with other couples for new sexual encounters). Another rumor was that I had run off with another man, abandoning my ten children. And of course, the standard rumor also circulated that we just couldn't live up to the standards of the Church and wanted to leave so we could "drink, and chew, and go out with people who do."

As is the case with LDS acquaintances, close friends fall into three categories:

1. The ones who tell you they love you no matter what, and although they're sad you don't believe in the Church any more, they are committed to keeping the relationship intact. It might only be a couple people; but you'll find these are real friends.

2. Those whose friendship is conditional upon your not talking about the reasons you left the Church or saying anything negative about it.

3. Those who find they can no longer associate with you. It could be because they're worried that being your friend would make them unworthy to hold a temple recommend (in the bishop's interview there's the question about associating or sympathizing with "apostates"). Or it could be that their spouse or parents forbid them from associating with you. Or it just might be that they feel personally rejected by your leaving the Church and that they have nothing in common with you anymore.

A good friend who was my 1st counselor in the Relief Society presidency, stopped keeping in contact with me—not of her own choice—but because of her husband's interference. Every time I dropped by her house, her husband told me she wasn't home. I would ask him to please tell her I stopped by and to have her call me. I never heard from her, so eventually I just assumed she wasn't interested in my friendship. I found out years later, after we reconnected on Facebook, that her husband never passed on any messages from me.

I had two close LDS friends outside the ward who are my friends to this day: LeAnne and my singing teacher Pat, with whom I'd been through thick and thin over the years. Although saddened that I "lost my testimony," they never stopped treating me any differently. Those are true friends. If you have any, cherish those friendships; they are rare.

Extended Family

Extended family includes in-laws, grown siblings, grandparents, aunts, uncles, and cousins. If you come from or married into a family with a strong LDS heritage, you can expect your relatives (in-laws and out-laws) to make concerted efforts to bring you back to the Church and "help" you regain your testimony. From my own experience and the stories I hear from ex-LDS, there seems to be three patterns of behavior, and the more LDS relatives you have, the greater the chance you'll observe all three reactions.

The first group consists of those who show genuine concern. They'll want to know your reasons for leaving and may try to convince you to not give up on the Church, but to keep praying and attending the temple. They'll try to point out why the things you've read are not credible (even though they've probably never read them, nor checked out the validity of the information for themselves). Their efforts will be fairly intense for a few months and then begin to dwindle. Even after this group of relatives stops actively trying to reconvert you, every time they call or see you they'll ask with great concern and pity in their eyes, "So how are you *really* doing?" As if you could not possibly be happy outside of the Church.

The second group of relatives will communicate and associate with you on the condition that you don't talk about why you left the Church. They don't want to hear anything negative or derogatory about the Church or its leaders, and they certainly don't wish to hear about any problems or discrepancies in Church history or doctrines. If ignorance was bliss they would be the happiest, most exuberant people on earth. They'll be more than eager to continue telling you about their callings or ward activities or the latest talks from General Conference, but they'll look at you glassy-eyed or be patronizing to you when you tell them about the Bible study you've been going to or the sermon your pastor preached that week. It's not that they're trying to be unkind or condescending, it's just that from their perspective you don't have the fullness of the gospel any longer, and the things you're learning in your new church or personal study are incomplete and not in accordance with the "restored gospel."

The third kind of response to expect from at least a few relatives is rejection, especially if you have your name removed from the records of the Church. They may tell you that you're no longer welcome in their homes and forbid you from contacting any of their children. You might find that birthday and Christmas cards are returned unopened. This treatment is extremely hurtful and sadly much too common. One would think if a person belonged to the Only True and Living Church upon the face of the earth, claiming to be a follower of Christ, that he or she would be *more* loving, *more* charitable, and *more* likely to demonstrate "the love of God." But, they are human (as are we), and often let emotions and pride get the best of them.

When we were in process of leaving the Church, there were a ton of devout family members on my then-husband's side of the family. Since I was an only child in a non-Mormon family, my parents and aunt were thankful I was quitting Mormonism. One of my cousins and her husband were inactive LDS and curious over why I was leaving the Church, but they never treated me any differently. They were interested in reading my "exit story," which I had put into booklet form. Their level of belief would classify them as cultural Mormons. They enjoyed the fellowship and community of Mormonism, but didn't really buy into the Joseph Smith story and all.

On my husband's side, however, their family lineage traced back to the days of Joseph Smith and the early Church. Their great-great-whatever-great grandfather was one of Smith's bodyguards. In fact, I've heard quite a few Mormons tell me about an ancestor who was one of

Smith's bodyguards. He seems to have needed quite a few of them on hand. Knowing the history of polygamy and Smith's teenage wives, and the wives he took from other men, it's no wonder he needed a whole regiment of bodyguards!

In my husband's immediate family there were 16 children. At the time we left the Church in 2000 and 2001 respectively, his parent's had 102 grandchildren. Ten of them were ours. I believe there has been one or two additions to the number of grandkids since then. With such a large extended family, we experienced a variety of reactions when we left.

Expect that some people in your family will assume you are leaving the Church because of sin or being offended. About three of Scott's siblings, a nephew, and his father tried to debate with us why the Church was true. They were convinced that if Scott would just "clean up his act and become worthy," then he could get his testimony back. Scott's response was that whether he was worthy or not had no bearing on the events of the past. Whether he went to the temple or not didn't change the fact that Joseph Smith took other men's wives as his own (11 of them), or used a "peep stone" instead of the purported Urim and Thummin to translate the elusory gold plates.

His brother, "Clarence" (name changed to protect the guilty), asked Scott during a visit, "What sins are you committing that are so great that it's causing you to doubt the Church?" Scott replied that he probably has a lot of sins, but that didn't change Church history.

It's rather interesting to me how his family interpreted our leaving the Church. The siblings in the previous paragraph were certain that Scott lost his testimony due to sin and that he could get it back by becoming temple-worthy. So, how did they think I lost my testimony? I was a temple-attending Relief Society president. I guess they either thought I was being deceived or that I had some unresolved sin from decades before. Who knows?

One sister and her husband confided that they weren't so sure the

Church was true either, but that it essentially was the best thing on the block so why not keep going (and pretending to believe it).

Another brother-in-law was of the opinion that the Church was true, but was operating under "fallen" or "uninspired" leadership. He said the Church was out of order and had been for many decades; however, when the Lord returns to the earth he would set his Church in order again after "cleaning house."

One of our nephews invited us to talk with his LDS institute director about the problems we discovered regarding Church history and practices. We were happy to do so for a couple reasons. My reason was to show my nephew and the institute director how false Mormonism was. I figured it was obvious now that we found and evaluated the evidence. Scott's reason for going was because he was hoping beyond hope that the Church was still true. He hoped the institute director would be able to provide rational explanations supported by facts for the discrepancies, changes, and what appeared to be cover-ups in Mormon history.

The other responses we got could be termed as "head in the sand syndrome." One brother outright told us not to tell him what we found out about the Church because he didn't want his testimony shaken. He didn't want to be confused with the facts.

One time Scott called his brother, Clarence, to talk about Mormonism. Clarence's wife answered the phone and said, "Scott, we think the world of you and we love you; but if you want to continue associating with us, we're going to have to ask you not to bring up any anti-Mormon subjects. Clarence was just made bishop of our ward and he needs to focus on his new calling."

Immediate Family

Now we come to the core group of individuals with whom you've established your own nuclear family. Whether you live at home with your parents or are living independently, your closest family members are probably parents and siblings. A note about being in a relationship will be included at the end of this section. Maybe you're married, with or without children. It's going to be difficult to break the news. However, you may be surprised and find that your spouse has had doubts all along but was afraid to say anything. Take courage!

I can do all things through Him who gives me power.
(Philippians 4:13).

Furthermore, we know that God causes everything to work together for the good of those who love God and are called in accordance with his purpose.
(Romans 8:28).

That is not to say that things will be easy or that they will turn out favorably or the way you want them to. This is to say that even through the most difficult circumstances God will give you the strength to endure them. In the end, those experiences will be worked together for our good, although we may not see how until much later.

Assuming you have an active TBM family, understandably, your spouse will be alarmed. If you were sealed in the temple, there will be major concern on your spouse's part over what impact your loss of testimony will have on being an "eternal family unit." They will have the same questions running through their minds as you have through yours; only from a different perspective: what will this mean for our marriage? How will this affect the kids? How will we handle matters of faith? What will we do about going to church?

Here are some of the potential outcomes of your announcement that you no longer support or believe in Mormonism:

A. Your spouse investigates your claims and exits the Church with you.
B. Your spouse investigates your claims and refuses to believe the evidence.

C. Your spouse refuses to look into your claims, but stays with you on condition that you don't discuss it.
D. Your spouse threatens to divorce you, or proceeds to divorce you.

In my situation, my husband had doubts about the Church and struggled with his testimony for years. He came to me with his doubts about seven or eight years before I left the Church. He found a book that had been thrown away somewhere (okay, I'll confess: Scott used to really enjoy dumpster-diving). It was the book by Charles Larson entitled *By His Own hand Upon Papyrus*. The author presented compelling evidence against the Church's claim that the Book of Abraham came from ancient documents purported to be written by the Biblical patriarch Abraham himself. It was this book—among other things—that caused Scott to be unsure about the credibility of Mormonism.

As he read the book he began telling me about it because he was disturbed the author's assertions. For days we had discussions about what we would do if the Church wasn't true. We were both very troubled and somewhat scared. If the Church wasn't true, then what was? It was just too much to take in. After three or four days of inner turmoil, I sat in the car and cried as I was about to do some grocery shopping. I remember this line of thinking: When I think about the Church not being true, I feel anxiety and have negative feelings. When I think about it being true, I feel calm and peaceful. Therefore, the Church must be true.

Later that evening when Scott began to share the latest chapter of the book with me, I stopped him. I said, "Scott, deep down inside I know the Church is true because I feel good when I think about it. I don't want you to tell me anymore about what you're reading. I'm really worried

about the kids, because what if the Church really is true—and I believe it is—and they lose their testimonies because of your doubts? What if they go astray and don't go on missions or get married in the temple? We won't be together for eternity."

Scott promised to keep his doubts to himself. And he did. He kept his word. He didn't say anything to the kids about his concerns. He kept faithfully attending the meetings with the family. We kept reading from the Book of Mormon and praying together daily as a family. Scott decided to just go on as if the Church was true because first, there was a possibility that it really was true; and second, even if it wasn't true it was still the best thing out there (or so he thought). He stopped bearing his testimony in church and at home, which saddened me because I wanted our kids to see a good, strong spiritual example from their father; but, I was thankful for his cooperation. That's how we handled the disparity in our beliefs for several years.

Your children's reactions will be determined by their ages. Adult children will have responses similar to extended family. On one end of the spectrum they might listen, do their own research, and come to the same conclusions as you; on the other end, they might cut off contact with you. Most ex-Mormons have experienced reactions from their adult children that fall somewhere in the middle. In other words, their kids don't follow them out of Mormonism, but neither do they cut off contact. Regardless of where these relationships ultimately end up, the transition period is always the roughest. This period of time can last from a few weeks to a few months, or to a few years in extreme cases, as you and your family come to terms with your decision to leave the Church and begin to work out the new dynamics of your relationships.

If you have teenagers, this will be hard on them. The teenage years can be tumultuous anyway, even if you have well-adjusted kids. They're at an age where they're trying to determine who they really are, what values they want to adopt, and what they really believe and stand for.

Now throw into the mix that everything that they had been taught was true, is now being questioned by the very person (or people) who led them along that spiritual path.

Most likely, the majority of your teen's peers are LDS. They all may regularly attend Young Men/Young Women activities, scouts, and seminary. News travels fast, especially when there's "apostasy" in the ranks. Your son's or daughter's friends might be asking if the rumors are true, leading to embarrassment or shame.

All their lives they've heard (and recited) the mantra, "I know the Church is true. I know Joseph Smith was a prophet. I know President (Whomever is leading the Church) is a prophet of God. I love my mom and dad (or youth leaders and friends). In the name of Jesus Christ, amen." All their lives they've been taught to trust their feelings in spiritual matters and that those feelings are actually promptings of the Spirit. Suddenly you're telling them that feelings are unreliable in matters of faith and they need to examine everything with their minds and reason. You can expect volatile reactions. Anticipate that they'll to go to Church leaders and ward members for guidance. There may be teary outbursts and heated exchanges. Expect tears. The whole atmosphere of your home can become tense and charged with emotional electricity.

Preteens and younger can usually be reasoned with. They'll follow your lead if things are handled well. If you stop attending the ward as a family, your children will certainly miss their friends, but if you explain that it's the teachings of the Church that you're rejecting—not LDS friends—it will be easier for them to accept.

For me, the greatest challenge in the year following my exit, was trying to convince my teenagers that I wasn't being led astray by Satan. I was inviting them to look at the evidence, to check things out for themselves, and to see if there was any validity to the claims I was making (and validity to the claims the Church was making), while ward leaders were telling them to avoid (so-called) anti-Mormon propaganda.

Every week when my husband and teens went to church, members would put their arms around their shoulders and express condolences, saying things like this:

"Your mom is just confused. She's being led astray by Satan."

"Just stay strong and keep praying for her. She'll come back."

"We've put your mom's name on the prayer roll at the temple."

There were ward members who pretended nothing had happened, and those who asked my husband with pity in their eyes, "So how is your wife doing, brother? She's just really confused now. We're so sorry." The funny thing is that Scott would tell people that I was doing great and was happier than ever, but they would just shake their heads sadly, grip his hand a little tighter, and ask again, "How is she *really* doing?"

This outreach is understandable from a Mormon perspective. In fact, it's understandable in any situation where someone leaves a deeply ingrained belief system. The people left behind have feelings too. Most of them feel genuine sorrow and concern, and a few feel anger and contempt.

Before exploring ways to break the news to your family, there are two special situations that should be addressed. The first situation is if you are dating or are engaged to a devout Latter-day Saint. It's very likely that your leaving the Church will be a deal-breaker. As hard as that is, it's not necessarily a bad thing. Better to deal with the situation now—before you're married and children come along—than after, when commitment and emotional and financial investment make exiting the Church much harder on the relationship.

Although this is disheartening news, there's also encouraging news. I'm aware of a couple where the man had just gotten home from his mission and began dating a young woman. Both were from strong LDS homes. They got engaged. Somewhere along the way, one of them ran across negative information about the Church, and they both decided to investigate further. They ended up leaving Mormonism together, got married, and now attend a non-denominational church.

A word of caution: do not keep your feelings or decision to leave the Church hidden until after the wedding, thinking you'll reveal things later and be able to convince him or her to leave the Church too. This is dishonest and unfair. Your fiancé/fiancée has expectations for your lives together based on a mutual religious perspective and shared beliefs. Springing your new beliefs on someone after you've tied the knot is nothing more than a "bait and switch tactic." Please, please don't do this, even if it means the engagement gets broken off.

Leaving Mormonism and converting to traditional Christianity or Messianic Judaism (or whatever else) is a life-changing event for yourself, as well as a possible gamer-changer for your betrothed. It's the kind of thing that will either make you or break you as a couple and should be worked through in advance of the nuptials.

The second special situation regards what you can expect from the LDS community at large should you decide to start a blog, write a book, or otherwise publicly announce your departure from and disagreement with Mormonism. The Church as an organization will ignore you. Most members don't make an effort to keep up with the latest news on the exodus of people leaving the Church. However, a small percentage of Mormons like to engage in apologetics defending Mormonism. Be prepared for personal attacks. Whether the mean, insulting, angry, or hateful comments are coming from real members of the Church or from internet trolls stirring up contention, reading derogatory comments directed at you can be hurtful and discouraging. Just know in advance that you'll be persona non grata in many LDS circles.

We've covered what you can expect from your loved ones and ward members. Let's move on to what your LDS loved ones can expect from *you*, and how to avoid the most common blunders.

2

Tossing Tact in the Toilet

"Don't Flatter Yourself that friendship authorizes you to say disagreeable things to your intimates. The nearer you come into relation with a person, the more necessary do tact and courtesy become."
~ Oliver Wendell Holmes

There is no one right way to tell your family and other Mormons in your life that you no longer believe and that you've found a new faith. What works for one person might not work for another. That being said, there are definitely *wrong* ways to tell people. What can happen when you not-so-tactfully blurt out that Joseph Smith was a "no-good so-and-so," compared to gently introducing facts and letting other people come to their own conclusions?

Question: What kinds of problems did leaving the Church cause in your marriage? How did your children react? How did extended family react?

Luckily I wasn't married when I left the church, and I [eventually] married a never-mo. Sometimes he doesn't understand were I'm coming from with doctrinal issues and/or why I think the way I do. Most of my family is still cordial with me, but we aren't as close anymore. Some of my cousins no longer speak to me.

My first husband didn't have much of a testimony of the church, and I think that caused a lot of problems in our marriage since he was supposed to be the priesthood holder and the patriarch of the family. I would take the kids to church by myself. I ended up leaving the Church at the same time we divorced. Our kids have been confused about religion since I push them towards Christianity, but their grandparents, aunts, uncles, and cousins keep trying to get them to go back to Mormonism.

I left 4 years ago, and am currently in a divorce after being married 45 years. One daughter who lives nearby will not let me see her six children unless I am accompanied. My other grown children with kids are not quite so bad, but I know they would not want me to be alone with their kids, even though I have told all that I will not bring up or discuss religion with them. Some of my children have left Mormonism, but are now complete atheists. My own family is not LDS, but 40-plus years of being LDS destroyed my relationships with them. Now that I have left, my relationships with his LDS family have greatly deteriorated.

No problems with my children. My fiancé at the time was on the path [out] with me. My extended family was never Mormon. I was lucky.

I was blessed because hubby and I left at the same time. We have a blended family, so his two boys can't deal with it. My 2 boys have left too, and many other family members.

My hubby had gone through the motions but never believed, so that was great.

I wasn't married, and my kids were little; but my family was disappointed.

Could things have turned out differently for the ex-Mormons quoted above? Who knows. It's easy to second-guess ourselves when things don't turn out the way we would have liked or when something goes wrong. We can live the rest of our lives beating ourselves up over "would've-should've-could've." But it isn't productive, useful, or healthy to live like that, always looking in the rear-view mirror of our past, and wishing we had done things differently. As they say, "Hindsight is 20/20." Just realize that even if you did things perfectly; even if you had said the right things in the right way at the right time, there's no assurance that everything would have been a bed of roses (without thorns).

Giving your family the news about your recent discoveries takes finesse and timing. I heard a joke a long time ago that now circulates on the internet:

> A man went on an extended vacation after asking his brother to take care of his cat while he was away. When the man returned, he called his brother to see if he could go pick up his beloved pet.
>
> His brother hesitated, and then blurted out, "I'm really sorry, but your cat is dead."
>
> "What!" His brother screamed into the phone. "You can't just

tell me like that! You should have broken it to me gently! When I first called, you should have said the cat is on the roof and you can't get her down. The next day you should have called me and said she fell off the roof, but the vet was patching her up. Then the day after that you could have given me the news that she didn't make it."

"I'm sorry," the brother apologized.

"Don't worry about it. By the way, how's Mom?"

"Well, she's on the roof and I can't get her down."

So what's the best way to break the news that your testimony is "on the roof and you can't get it down?" I can tell you how *not* to do it, with examples from my own exit. I'll put it like this: my initials, T.T., do not stand for Tactful Tracy.

My husband and I were on the same path out of the Church, although I was farther ahead in terms of wanting to make a clean break. We were both studying and reading like crazy. Scott had a pile of books he was reading, and I had my own. We stayed up night after night until past midnight, spending time reading, and on the internet researching and learning.

At first we weren't quite ready to tell the kids because it had not yet been settled in our minds that the Church wasn't true, and we didn't want to take a chance of damaging their budding testimonies in case we were wrong. Finally, when it was clear to me that Mormonism was a sham, I couldn't stop telling people. I began reading the Bible and listening to commentaries on cassette tape. I stopped believing in the god of Mormonism, an exalted man who was once like us on some other world, worked his way to godhood, and was married to probably countless goddess wives who pumped out spirit babies like there was no tomorrow. I fully believed that was the truth all the time I was LDS.

I began to develop faith in the God of Abraham, Isaac, and Jacob;

the God who revealed himself in a pillar of fire by night and a glorious cloud by day to the Children of Israel. As I took that journey out of the religion of Joseph Smith and into the gospel proclaimed in the Bible, it was like a fog lifted from off my mind and I could think clearly for the first time in years. I was seeing everything in a new light, and it was great.

I supposed (naively and incorrectly) that all it would take for my LDS relatives, friends, and ward members to see that we had all been duped into believing the Mormon Church was true, was to just tell them the shocking facts, along with my uncensored and inflammatory commentary.

Every day for a week I called one sister-in-law with whom I was close (not any more, by the way; I alienated her) and said things like this:

> *Wow! You'll never believe what I just found out! Joe Smith was taking wives as young as 14 years old! What a pervert! Eleven of his wives still had husbands! He was actually schtooping other men's wives! He wasn't a prophet; he was a horn-dog!*
>
> *And Brigham Young; wow, what a corrupt man! He was evil. Did you know that he was responsible for the murder of over 120 men, women, and children in 1857? It was called the Mountain Meadows Massacre. He sure was a "liar, liar with his eternal pants on fire."*
>
> *Oh, and President Hinckley. There's a guy I always felt uneasy about. I don't know; there was just something about him that didn't feel right. Talk about a false prophet. Did you ever hear about the Salamander letters?*
>
> *And did you know this, and did you know that, and blah blah blah...*

A few months after my exit from Mormonism, the Young Women's advisor dropped by the house to pick up my 15-year-old daughter for an activity. As an aside, I refused to give my kids rides *to* church. I told them I would pick them up, but I could not in good conscience take them there. On this occasion I went out to the driveway to say hello to Sister McCormick, and she told me how much she missed seeing me at church. I don't remember how it came up, but I told her I could no longer believe in a "Jesus" that was conceived by Heavenly Father having sex with Mary. She responded by saying that the Church doesn't teach that. I gave her the references. She left in tears.

The General Authorities and Quorum of the Twelve Apostles were fair game for humor (or what *I* believed to be humor). If it was General Conference weekend and my older kids and their friends were talking about how inspirational it was, I could be overheard saying things like this:

I wonder what was Maxwell's magnanimous message to Mormons in meeting this morning (Neal A. Maxwell was known for his use of alliteration).

What did Thomas S. Monson talk about? Did he tell about the time he was a young bishop of a ward full of widows, and how he walked ten miles uphill—both ways—in the blinding snow, carrying three of them piggyback to church because they didn't have transportation?

Did they warn about the perils of drinking coffee and how it will spur members on to a life of crime and debauchery?

And just to be sure my kids knew where I stood, I made a sign that I hung on my closet door. I modified an expression from the then-popular Star Trek series in reference to the Borg (an alien race that takes over the minds of other species and connects them to the collective, or "hive mind," stripping them of their individuality and self-will). I saw a great similarity: Mormonism + Borg = Morg. My sign read:

We are the Morg.
Resistance is futile.
You will be assimilated.

I went out and got personalized license plates for my minivan: **XLDS4JC** and had a custom frame made with the message: **Ex-Mormon Because Truth Matters.**

I certainly wasn't following Dale Carnegie's advice on "How to Win Friends and Influence People." I was losing LDS friends left and right, and if I influenced them at all it was to avoid me at all costs.

If the poetess Elizabeth Barrett Browning was an ex-Mormon, she may have penned the following lines;

How do I alienate thee? Let me count the ways.
I alienate thee to the depth and breadth and height
My snarky comments can reach, when feeling you're out of sight...

In *my* mind I thought I became funny and clever, like; "How interesting! People who leave the Church become comedians!" Looking back, I see that in some respects I became the kind of person Mormons are warned about; someone who leaves the Church and becomes bitter and angry. Thus, the conclusion is drawn that the Church is true, because those who apostatize become not-so-very-nice-people. (But funny.)

Their conclusion is wrong that bad behavior on the part of defectors proves the veracity of Mormonism; but they are correct in saying that many do become bitter or angry, at least temporarily. There is a reason for this; anger is part of the grieving process.

The late psychiatrist Elisabeth Kübler-Ross theorized that there are five stages of grief individuals go through after some type of loss. Her studies revolved around death and dying, but a loss of any significance can evoke the same responses. The five stages are:

- Denial and isolation
- Anger
- Bargaining (includes "if only")
- Depression
- Acceptance

When a person comes to the conclusion that everything they believed about themselves and the world around them is false, it's a loss of identity. Follow that with all the repercussions from leaving the group or belief system—loss of relationships, culture, traditions, and confidence—and it's easy to see how an ex-Mormon can experience some or all of the reactions outlined in the stages of mourning.

Anger in former Mormons isn't limited to being the result of grief; it also stems from the sense of betrayal by leadership (the First Presidency and Quorum of the Twelve) who would have to be aware of the real history of the Church and yet continue to perpetuate disinformation and misinformation that faithful members base critical decisions on. Anyone would be upset believing that organizational heads of any entity (whether public, private, corporate, or religious) are taking advantage of people or misleading them. If "truth in advertising" applies to businesses, why doesn't it apply to businesses operating under the guise of religious organizations? The anger felt by former LDS is understandable given these conditions.

As devout Mormons our most important and life-changing decisions were based on our belief that Mormonism, along with all its auxiliaries and functions, was true. We made decisions based on patriarchal and priesthood blessings in terms of vocation, marriage and number of children, health, education, and more. My sister-in-law died from cancer as a result of refusing medical treatment because of several priesthood blessings that promised her faith alone would heal her.

I personally know two women (still members of the Church) who gave up their babies as unwed mothers when they might otherwise have wanted to raise them. They put their babies up for adoption through LDS Social Services because priesthood leaders told them it was "Heavenly Father's" will. Imagine giving up your child because you thought the Church was true and your bishop told you that your baby—that precious "pre-existent spirit"—was meant to go to another home all along. Then you later find out the Church isn't true. Imagine the pain and anger you would feel! Whether or not it would have been for the best is a moot point. They put their babies up for adoption through LDS Social Services only because the First Presidency of the Church, without knowing their personal circumstances, declared it was God's will.

Perhaps as an ex-Mormon you're coming to terms with choices you made while believing the Church was true. Although anger, resentment, and sadness are natural responses to discovering Mormonism (or some other worldview you totally believed) is false, if you don't take steps to work through the negative emotions they can consume you and lead to depression, broken relationships, poor health, and general unhappiness. In that state of mind, it's easy to make mistakes after leaving the Church. If you want to avoid damaging your relationships with LDS family and friends, here are the biggies to avoid:

- Angry outbursts
- Sarcasm
- Mocking
- Joking about what the other person believes is sacred
- Vulgarity
- Insensitivity
- Forcing the issue

- Disrespecting the other person's beliefs or requests
- Crossing boundaries
- Arguing
- Name calling
- Arrogance or superiority
- Bad attitude
- Threatening or trying to manipulate your spouse

Of course, steering clear of these behaviors goes both ways. LDS loved ones have no more business resorting to unkind and angry words and actions than does the person leaving the Church. When someone leaves Mormonism while other family members still believe, it's stressful on all sides, leading people to do things they wouldn't do under normal conditions, including saying things that are later regretted. Sometimes the issue isn't just what we say, but how often we say it. A temptation exists to do too much negative talking and becoming motor-mouths of the worst kind.

3

Motor-Mouth Mama

"Tact is the art of making a point without making an enemy."
~ Sir Isaac Newton

I couldn't stop telling people why Mormonism wasn't true whether they wanted to know or not, whether they were interested or not, or whether they were Mormons or not. No one was exempt from hearing about it, not even people on the street. One time as I was driving down a major road in North Las Vegas, I saw two LDS missionaries talking to a guy wearing a sandwich board advertising something at the corner of an intersection. I could see that they handed him what looked like a Book of Mormon. Naturally I thought it was a great opportunity to set things straight, so I made a u-turn (legally, of course), drove back to the parking lot close to the guy, and waited until the missionaries got on their bicycles and pedaled away. There was landscaping between me and him, so I leapt over a few bushes, climbed over a short retaining wall, swept my disheveled hair from my face, and approached the man.

"Hello!" I greeted warmly. "How are you? I noticed those two

Mormon missionaries talking to you. Are you Mormon?" He said he wasn't, so I continued. "Well, I used to be Mormon. I was LDS for 26 years and I just found out that the Church isn't true and that the Book of Mormon is a fraud. I just wanted to give you something to read that shows the other side." At this point I whipped out a copy of my exit-story which I had printed out and made into a booklet at Office Depot. I carried stacks of them in my vehicle wherever I went, just for occasions like this. The man thanked me and I left feeling happy that I may have prevented another spiritual casualty.

Besides telling people why the Church was false, I ranted and raved a lot. I always had some sarcastic remark waiting to be said either under my breath or loud enough to be heard. For example, if my TBM nieces were visiting and they said something to my LDS kids about a conference talk they just heard—maybe on "following the brethren"—then I'd say something like, "Oh yes. We really must believe and obey *everything* the brethren say. Heaven forbid we should have any thoughts of our own or use common sense."

I cringed every time someone from the ward saw me and greeted me as "Sister." I kept thinking, I am not your spirit sister; never was, never will be. And I would greet them in return by using their first name (or no name). If I had to introduce one of my children to a Mormon it was as "Mr. or Mrs." I was adamant about not pretending to be something I wasn't.

If anyone asked me how I was doing, somehow I was able to tie the answer to my leaving the Church; "I'm great, now that I'm not Mormon anymore," or "I'm much happier since becoming a Christian."

Talk about diarrhea of the mouth! I dropped a truckload everywhere I went. Oddly enough, this did not sit well with the LDS people in my life. Imagine that. In the following years, as I began to meet and know other ex-Mormons, I saw a lot of things that actually undermined their efforts to bring their family members out of Mormonism. I've heard of the new

Christian partner leaving gospel tracts in obvious places throughout the house, while the LDS partner left Ensign Magazines or conference talks about apostasy or strengthening one's testimony sitting in plain view. Besides reading material, spouses engaged in auditory assault. One person made sure to have a Christian radio station blaring in the house, and the LDS driver would be sure to have the Mormon Tabernacle Choir playing in the car; each side trying to convert (or aggravate) the other.

There's a big problem in human relationships, religion aside, and it's basically talking too much and listening too little. We want so desperately for our own views to be heard and understood, that we often forget that other people feel the same way and have the same needs to be heard and understood.

> ***A fool takes no pleasure in trying to understand; he only wants to express his own opinion.***
>
> *Proverbs 18:2*

Proverbs warns; "A fool takes no pleasure in trying to understand; he only wants to express his own opinion" (Proverbs 18:2).

"To answer someone before hearing him out is both stupid and embarrassing" (Proverbs 18:13).

Getting into endless arguments over which view is right is fruitless and harms the most important relationships you have: marital and parental. Mutual love and respect go far in preparing hearts to listen.

I had a friend who left the Church while he was the ward gospel doctrine teacher. He came across so-called anti-Mormon literature and set out to prove it wrong. Instead, he found that the information was accurate. Understandably, his wife was upset; so much so, that everything turned into an argument. For almost ten years they fought and argued, screaming at each other and cursing one another. When my friend tried to reason with his wife, asking her to just look at the evidence—that's all he asked, that she would just look—his wife refused to even consider any viewpoint other than her own. She was certain that anything putting Mormonism in a negative light was a pack of lies straight from hell.

Finally, when their animosity for each other became unbearable, they divorced. A few months later, my friend's ex-wife called him and asked for some of the websites and information he had researched about Mormonism. It wasn't long before they were meeting weekly to study the Bible together. The ex-wife finally consented to visit Dennis and Rauni Higley of H.I.S. Ministries International (a ministry outreach for questioning Mormons) and listen to what they had to say. With the overwhelming evidence against Mormonism from official Church books and manuals set before her, she could no longer accept that the Church was true. Within six months this couple remarried one another, equally yoked in the Christian faith. Miracles can happen once people overcome their pride.

4

Smoking, Drinking, and Prostituting on Street Corners

"When I read about the evils of drinking, I gave up reading."
~ Henny Youngman

Mormons have the tendency to believe a variation of the quote by Henny Youngman; essentially that when a weak Mormon hears about the evils of drinking (or living a riotous life) he gives up the Church, ostensibly because the standards are too hard to live up to. Although this couldn't be further from the truth, it's the perception.

In one of the wards we attended, I heard that a young mother I used to visit-teach had left the Church. All I knew was that I hadn't seen her at church for months, although her husband and kids still came. I thought that was sad, of course, but I never asked for the details. One day I ran up to the grocery store to pick up a few items, and lo and behold; there was Lisa in one of the aisles (might have been the coffee aisle) wearing shorts almost to her butt cheeks, high heels, and a tight top that showed some remarkable cleavage. She seemed surprised to see me and we just stood there awkwardly looking at each other for a moment. Finally, I asked her how things were going and told her how good it was to see her again.

When I got home I could hardly wait to tell my husband. "You'll never guess who I saw at the store today. Lisa 'So-and-so.' She was dressed like a prostitute. Guess she left the Church so she could drink coffee and sleep around."

One time we visited friends from a ward we previously were members of and asked for the latest news. They said that Brother and Sister So-and-so (no relation to Lisa So-and-so above) had gotten divorced. Bob just up and left his family and the Church. Not long afterward I went to the LDS credit union to make a deposit and there at the counter stood Bob and some woman. She was dressed in a mini-skirt, fishnet stockings, high heels, and a sleeveless blouse with some pretty remarkable cleavage showing. When I got home I dutifully reported to my husband that I saw Bob at the credit union with some floozy dressed like a prostitute. I guessed that was why he left the Church; so he could drink coffee and sleep around.

As they say, what goes around comes around. Eventually, when I left the Church and bought a coffee maker and tea kettle the day after I turned in my official resignation letter, my daughter was sure the next step for me was to become a prostitute. She cried, "You're drinking tea and coffee now! What could possibly come next?"

Little did she know it was already worse; much worse. I had a six-pack of beer hidden in my closet. And then I was introduced to the pleasures of Mike's Hard Lemonade and caramel macchiato lattes. Oddly enough, I never did develop an interest in smoking or prostitution.

Over the following three years I threw decorum out the window (hand in hand with tact). Not only did I start wearing sleeveless shirts and miniskirts, but I made sure to sport tight tank tops with ample cleavage showing and shorts that one should probably not bend over with. The worst part was that I made a special effort to wear that kind of clothing when I knew ward members would see me. I wanted them to see how much freedom I had as a "Christian." We could do all kinds of things as Christians—drink coffee, tea, and beer, and dress like hookers—and still go to heaven. Booyah!

I'm not proud of the way I behaved, and I'm sorry for the poor example I was of someone who claimed to "know the real Jesus." I was an in-your-face-ex-Mormon to the hilt! I've since learned not to be brazen simply for the sake of brazenness.

> *Just because you can, doesn't mean you should.*

As a former LDS, you're going to make mistakes. You'll feel conflicting emotions and some confusion. That's normal. All my mistakes were common behavior for someone coming out of a strict, conformist religious background. Mormonism isn't the only religious organization with narrowly-defined rules for worthiness or being considered a good member. Every major religion has certain sects that control the lives of its followers to a greater degree than others. People leaving those groups have a tendency to go to the opposite extreme or go through an adolescent phase. This is a common psychological reaction, so don't beat yourself up if down the road you look back with regret over how you acted right after you left Mormonism. Knowing these things in advance, however; knowing what's possible (and likely), it might be that you can spare yourself and your loved ones some of the negative aspects associated with leaving the Church.

If your spouse, children, roommate, parents, or whomever you're living with are still TBM's, keeping a fridge well-stocked with beer and wine is not going to be conducive to peace or to credible evangelism. As well, if you now identify yourself as a follower of the biblical Jesus but you're offending your loved ones left and right—not for the sake of Christ, but for the sake of personal freedom—then you will be a "stumbling block" for them. In retrospect, I think my children who eventually left Mormonism did so *in spite of* my example, not because of it.

Flaunting your new lifestyle in an arrogant manner in front of LDS friends and acquaintances like I did, is disrespecting their beliefs. Keep in mind that you once believed as they do and that which they believe to be sacred you did also. Mutual respect not only goes a long way in mending broken relationships, but it also invites others to understand your perspective as you seek to understand theirs. Understanding does not mean you have to agree.

I'm ashamed of this now, but at my son's missionary farewell open house I used passive resistance to thumb my nose at Mormonism by making a chili recipe that called for 12-oz of beer. Almost all the LDS guests commented on how it was some of the best chili they'd ever tasted (which gave me a perverse sense of satisfaction). When they asked what I put in it, I just smiled and told them it was a secret ingredient.

I'm sure many Mormons feel perfectly comfortable cooking with wine or beer in certain dishes, knowing the alcohol cooks out. Many of them would not have a problem enjoying dessert that calls for alcohol, such as Cherries Jubilee or Bananas Foster á la flambé. Still, my motivation was wrong and consequently disrespectful.

As you enjoy new experiences that conflict with Mormon standards—whether it's wearing a tank top on a hot summer day or having a glass of wine with your evening meal—let it be done in a way that honors the people around you. Honoring or respecting an individual as a human being is not the same as honoring a religious institution. If your spouse is still a devout Mormon and has asked you to please not drink alcoholic beverages in front of the family, when you respect that request you're honoring the marital relationship. You're not giving honor to a religious rule you don't agree with; you're submitting yourself to your spouse out of love, and out of love for the Lord.

Submit to one another in fear of the Messiah.
Ephesians 5:21

Just as the Messianic Community submits to the Messiah,
so also wives should submit to their husbands in everything.
As for husbands, love your wives, just as the Messiah
loved the Messianic Community; indeed, gave himself up on its
behalf, in order to set it apart for God...
Ephesians 5:25-26

This is how husbands ought to love their wives—
like their own bodies;
for the man who loves his wife is loving himself.
Ephesians 5:28

There is profound truth hidden here, which I say concerns the
Messiah and the Messianic Community. However, the text also
applies to each of you individually: let each man love his wife as he
does himself, and see that the wife respects her husband.
Ephesians 5:32-33

Adhere to the godly wisdom of the Apostle Paul. I encourage you to be sensitive to the feelings of those closest to you and over whose relationships you have a stewardship.

5

Living in Fear and Regret

"I learned that courage was not the absence of fear, but the triumph over it. The brave man is not he who does not feel afraid, but he who conquers that fear."
~ Nelson Mandela

One of the biggest challenges faced by former Mormons as we discover the Church isn't what it claimed to be, is fear. We're afraid of the unknown; afraid of where the discovery of its falsehood will lead us. We're afraid of what it might mean for our relationships, daily lives, and perhaps our jobs (if at an LDS-owned business) or school (if a student at BYU or satellite campus). We might even live in fear of being deceived again. We're often afraid to tell the significant others in our lives that we don't believe the Church is true anymore or that we've "lost" our testimonies. How will we break the news to our Bishops that we want to be released from our callings? How will we respond to awkward phone calls and visits by ward members and home teachers who ask why we haven't been coming to church?

In the survey I asked;

What was the worst part about leaving Mormonism? The best part? How long did it take you to recover from life as a Mormon?

The worst part was losing family and friends. The best part was being born again and knowing Jesus. I left the Church 6 years ago and am still recovering.

Worst part: Friends turning their backs on me without understanding or trying to understand. They never loved me, and that hurt.
Best part: I wasn't living a lie!
I will never be fully recovered. I will always be wary of trusting a church again.

The worst part was the reaction from my husband and children. They think I'm following Satan, that someday I will come back, and that I am an apostate. Destroying my family, couldn't attend my youngest daughter's temple wedding, and feeling so alone.
The first year was a complete nightmare. The second was still bad, but not as bad as the first. The third was still difficult in many ways. The best part is that it has been four years now, and I am finally getting over Mormonism!

I still feel very angry for being mislead for so many years, and I feel devastated that I taught my children to believe in it! We sent 8 missionaries out through the years, and the other 2 of our children were married in the temple (I have 7 boys, 3 girls; all the boys served missions, and one of the girls. Now I have missionary grandchildren). There are consequences that will go on for the rest of my life, and recovery is ongoing.

The best part was realizing I was out of the lies and deceits of Mormonism! I no longer felt guilty. I felt spiritually fed every Sunday, enjoying Sundays finally, loving being back in God's Word, studying and hearing about Jesus Christ, talking about Jesus Christ, and learning more and more every day. I feel like I have 45+ years of missed learning opportunities, as far as true teachings. The best part is feeling the love and forgiveness of Jesus Christ.

The worst part of leaving was the loss of my identity. It was so wrapped up in Mormonism that I was a bit lost and lonely, until a new Christian friend told me all I ever had to be was a "new creation in Christ." She said to rest [take comfort] in that for a while and it would eventually become clear. She was so right. I guess I had been kept so busy doing stuff for "the Church." Then all of a sudden I had time to relax and contemplate.

Well, at first I watched a video called The Bible vs. The Book of Mormon that someone gave me out of love. I was convinced and convicted the moment I saw it! I knew instantly I had been lied to for 42 years. I was married in the Temple, and lived all of it [Mormonism]. I worked through some of the negative emotions and was mad a few times for being lied to, but we began attending Calvary Church, with a great—and Biblically literate—teacher. It was Bible-only teachings! This was my saving grace at the time; now I know it's Jesus my Savior who pulled me through.

I missed the LDS community and the chance to do service so often, but I liked the freedom and love I've felt from God since leaving. It's only been 6 months, but I think I'm doing pretty good.

Worst part about leaving Mormonism is the initial loneliness and feeling like no one has ever been through what you are going through.
The best part is freedom in Christ and no worry of needing to be good enough or worthy enough.
I am still recovering, and I'm sure I probably will be the rest of my life. I was "born in the covenant," so even though I left Mormonism, it's still part of my heritage.

For me, the worst part was knowing I had unwittingly led my children astray all those years. I taught them to rely on their feelings to discern spiritual truth. Whenever they'd have a good, warm feeling I would explain that it was the "Holy Ghost" testifying to them that something was true. Ugh! The reality is that all those warm fuzzy feelings were no different than what we felt after watching heart-warming movies like Steven Spielberg's *E.T. the Extra-Terrestrial.* Did that mean the "Spirit" was confirming that aliens were real? I think not.

I also felt bad for all the wasted time, the 26 years of my life serving a god that didn't even exist. I thought of all the needless risks I took with my health and life over the years because my Patriarchal Blessing said I would be "blessed with health and strength" and live in the flesh to see the Second Coming of Christ. I did a lot of things I would never have done had I known I wasn't invincible. After leaving the Church I got really upset about it, thinking of how I could be dead because I believed some priesthood blessing that amounted to nothing more than fortune-telling at worst and story-telling at best.

Over my years as a Mormon, I felt like I didn't quite fit in with most ward members anyway; so losing my LDS "friends" wasn't really a big deal. But it did hurt that some of them thought the worst of me: that I left the Church to drink, smoke, and prostitute on street corners. I'm sort of joking, although a few people actually thought worse things. An LDS nephew told me the rumor going around extended family was that Scott and I left the Church because we were "swingers." Ouch.

For me, the best part of leaving the LDS Church and coming to biblical faith was the almost immediate sense of relief. It was like a burden was completely lifted off my shoulders.

For the first time in my life I understood that no one can ever be worthy or good enough by their own efforts and merit. This is why God sent the Messiah, His unique Son, to redeem those who repent and trust on his righteousness. In other words, the day to day struggle of doing enough good works to earn God's favor was over. I was set free. I no longer had to question if I was worthy enough or good enough or doing enough. Not only was I spiritually set free, but physically as well. The back pain I had suffered from for years left me. One morning I woke up and noticed that I could bend down and tie my shoes without great effort. I was also able to bend over the crib to lay the baby down, instead of leaning forward as much as possible and kind of plopping her onto the mattress, which had to be adjusted to the highest position.

> *Come to me, all of you who are struggling and burdened, and I will give you rest. Take my yoke upon you and learn from me, because I am gentle and humble in heart, and you will find rest for your souls. For my yoke is easy, and my burden is light.*
>
> Matthew 11:28-30

The best part about leaving Mormonism was learning that the gospel wasn't a system or methodology to advance oneself toward godhood. No, the gospel is the good news that the kingdom of God is here through Messiah and we have the opportunity to be engaged in good works in response to our salvation, not as a means to achieve salvation. It brings me great joy to see most of my ten children and grandchildren trusting in the God of Abraham, Isaac, and Jacob and believing that he is fulfilling his promise to redeem mankind through the Messiah Yeshua (Christ Jesus).

Ex-Mormons live with a lot of fear and regret. Often we're stalled in moving forward by self-recrimination; *if only, I should have known, why did I, why didn't I*, and other unproductive recurring thoughts. This phase is the most intense during the first couple months and years after exiting Mormonism and fades over time as we begin to see with new eyes and clearer perspectives.

Fear can take many forms. It can be fear of how our loved ones will react, fear of rejection, or fear of losing our most important relationships. Fear can keep us from meeting new people and making new friends. We might be held back by a fear of the future because everything seems so uncertain. Fear of being deceived again can cause a former Mormon to be skeptical of all religion. Many ex-LDS have flashes of fear that we made the wrong choice to leave the Church. An overwhelming panic makes us question; *What if the Church is true after all? Am I going to "Outer Darkness?"Did I condemn my children to hell by leaving the Church? What if all that anti-Mormon stuff was made up by enemies of the Church?*

Fortunately, those anxiety attacks get fewer and farther in-between until one day we realize our fear has been replaced by indescribable peace. I no longer ever wonder if Mormonism is really true. That it wasn't established by God is as evident to me as the sun shining at noon (with or without cloud cover).

Regret is another hindrance to healing and recovery. Whether we're regretting wasted time, effort, money, or the way we did or didn't handle things, it isn't a healthy way to live and will not facilitate recovery. Continually living in the past or condemning ourselves for mistakes we've made leads to depression, isolation, and poor health. Doing so keeps us from productive living, keeping us withdrawn instead of fully enjoying the relationships we still have with loved ones.

It takes time to learn new things, to develop a different worldview, to sort out what values we want to keep and what ones we don't. There's a danger of throwing out all the good that we learned as Mormons simply because we've come to the conclusion Mormonism isn't true. If the Church taught 2 + 2 = 4, should we stop believing in correct math principles just because other teachings were false? The Church may teach false things about its origins, but that doesn't mean that everything coming over the LDS pulpit is wrong. Keep the good, throw out the bad.

It took me a long time to feel comfortable acknowledging the good things that came from my 26 years as a Mormon. For the first dozen years after I left, I didn't want to give credit to Mormonism for anything because I didn't want to offend God. However, as my spiritual walk matured and as I began to study more diligently, I began to see that God allows all kinds of experiences into our lives for a reason, even things that are painful. He uses both good and bad for our personal growth and to increase our trust in him.

I heard a Messianic Jewish teacher speak at a seminar. A "Messianic Jew," is a Jewish person who believes that Jesus (Yeshua) is the promised Messiah, while still maintaining Jewish identity and practice. He talked about "giving honor where honor is due." He used Scripture, as well as rabbinical teachings, to explain how honoring and respecting others honors God. I asked him if that meant giving honor or credit to people who positively influenced our lives even if they weren't believers. I told him that I didn't want to give any credit to a religious organization that taught a false gospel.

He explained that God instructs us to give honor where it's due. So, if we had an elementary school teacher who made a difference in our lives, we should give honor and respect to the individual. It could have been an employer, a co-worker, a neighbor, or a family member who taught us something important and valuable. In Pirkei Avot 6:3 (collection of rabbinical teachings on ethics) we read;

> Whoever learns from someone else a single chapter, a single verse, a single word, even a single letter, must treat him with honor, for so we find in the case of David, king of Israel, who learned only two things from Ahitophel, yet called him his teacher, his guide, and his close friend, for so it says, "But it is you, my equal, my guide, my close friend" [Psalm 55:13]. The following inference can be derived: if David, king of Israel, who learned only two things from Ahitophel, called him his teacher, guide, and close friend, how much more must one who learns from someone else a chapter, a verse, a word, or even a single letter, treat him with honor! And honor is due only to Torah [the law of God or God's instructions], as it is written, "The wise shall inherit honor" [Proverbs 3:35], and "The wholehearted attain good," and "good" signifies Torah, as it is said, "I have given you good instruction, do not forsake my Torah" [Proverbs 4:2].

The Messianic teacher asked me if any Mormons taught me anything good during my life. I said yes; that while many of the Church's doctrines are wrong, I learned good values, among other important things. He then told me that I can honor the Mormons who made a difference in my life as individuals, without giving honor to a false religion.

He asked, "How do you know that HaShem (Hebrew title for God, meaning *The Name*) didn't put these people into your life to teach you something or change you in some way? Maybe he used your time in the Mormon Church to accomplish his purposes."

This man's words not only blessed me and gave me greater insight into God's ways, but his message freed me on some level. Now I can look back with gratefulness instead of regret. I can say thank you to the bishops, Young Women's advisors, and Relief Society presidents I

personally knew who were people of good character ar
thank the LDS women in my life who exemplified cha
and who taught me how to be a better wife, mother, and homema

Because of my membership in the LDS Church I was afforded opportunities to develop public speaking and teaching skills. I was able to sing and perform in front of thousands of people over the years in different meetings and conferences I was invited to participate in. Because of various leadership positions I was called to, I learned how to lead and delegate. I learned the values of teamwork, service, and diligence. I even learned how to lead music.

I can be thankful for my ten amazing children! I'm sure I wouldn't have had ten kids if it hadn't been for my beliefs as a Mormon. I love every single one of them so much, and looking back I wish I had a couple more kids after leaving the Church, even though there weren't any "spirit children" in heaven waiting to come down for "their turn on earth."

There's so much to be grateful for, even with all the negatives associated with leaving the Church. Loss of friends, temporary loss of identity, ugly false rumors, character attacks; all these things have brought a significant amount of pain into my life, but they are nothing compared to the joy and blessing of knowing the True and Living God.

Now I can give honor where it's due, and it's hard to describe how good that feels, especially when I recognize God's hand on my life. I don't have to be *bitter* when I can be *better* by trusting in God's plans and instruction.

I've made new friends. I have a sense of purpose and mission again. I have hope. I have Life.

Don't let fear and regret paralyze you and keep you from truly living.

6

Isolating Yourself

"Loneliness and the feeling of being unwanted
is the most terrible poverty."
~ Mother Teresa

After leaving the Church it's common to experience loneliness, self-doubt, depression, and apprehension. The longer you were a believing Mormon, the more intense these feelings will be. It's crucial to your mental and emotional health to take steps toward recovery as soon as possible. Try not to isolate or distance yourself from others, especially from those who would be a support and strength to you.

You're not alone. The internet makes it possible for a wide variety of people and resources to be available to help you in your journey to reality. Unless you live in an area where the LDS Church doesn't have a visible presence, there are probably a significant number of ex-Mormons within a 25-mile radius of you. Meet-up groups for ex-Mormons, forums, chat-groups, Facebook groups, and other ways to connect with recovering ex-Mo's abound.

Following are some of the responses received from the survey:

What things helped you as you were leaving the Church and afterward? What encouragement or advice would you like to pass on?

Finding groups of ex-Mormon Christians (mainly online forums or Facebook) and talking to people about common experiences. My prayer life, reading the Bible, and my relationship with Christ has helped a lot too. Christ can heal all things.

My advice is to please don't think you are alone. Find other ex-Mormons and interact with them, talk to them, ask questions. The ex-Mormon community is extremely loving and accepting, and you will be welcomed as you are. We want to help you grow and recover from Mormonism.

Support groups where I could openly ask questions. Seek always. Ask questions. If you don't or you're afraid certain things are off limits, you'll get stuck and lose sight of things.

Go to a Biblical church, and if you can't find one in your area, find one online. We listen to Pastor Greg Laurie every week on CSN radio online. Music is a huge part of my walk with Christ! Worshiping Jesus through music has made all the difference.

The Lady's Bible study groups were wonderful! I made new female friends, and learned so much about the Bible and who God really is. I suggest writing down what you discover about the wrong doctrines of Mormonism to refer back to, and a letter explaining why you left. It may take two years to write it, and that's OK; but then eventually you can just keep a copy to hand to anyone who asks. That way they can take it with them to read calmly later. It's easier than trying to keep them on target. Mormons tend to end the discussion as soon as it makes them uncomfortable. They go off to another rabbit hole and nothing gets finished getting explained.

Ex-mo books, Facebook groups, the Bible, Bible studies, and the Baptist Church is what helped me the most.

Listening to Christian music and reading the Word have helped. Surrounding myself with other ex-Mormons who have become Christians has helped a lot.

Reading the Bible, praying, being with Christians, going to church, and studying. Although I did read plenty of history about the LDS Church, I am still really saddened or depressed when I read yet another book. I feel it is more healing to study, pray, and live among Christians than it is to dwell on the negative things of Mormonism.

I feel we have to maintain respect toward our friends and family members who are LDS, remembering how we felt when we were active members. I don't believe we can convert Mormons, but that it will take the Lord drawing them to himself. All we can do is pray and be the best examples we can, trying to be loving and uncontentious.

Steps to recovery don't have to include immediately finding a different church. Go at your own pace. You might not feel comfortable getting involved in other religious activities, and that's okay. Whether or not you decide to begin attending Christian or Messianic church services right away, it's very beneficial and healing to connect with other former

Mormons. These are people who can relate to what you're going through and can provide the support and understanding you need.

A good support group provides a safe environment to express your feelings and frustrations—and yes—even anger at the LDS Church without being criticized for it. Humor often alleviates some of the stress. Just remember to keep the humor within the group and not expressed to your LDS family and friends. You'll meet people with similar experiences who can tell you what worked for them and what didn't. Not all support groups are alike. Some groups are definitely secular and may include language you don't feel comfortable with. Some ex-LDS forums are slanted toward atheism and many posts are derogatory and critical of God, religion, and faith in general. So just be aware. Fortunately, there are enough support groups out there for everyone to find what's best suited for their personal needs.

A good support group provides a safe environment to express your feelings and frustrations.

When I left Mormonism, I "went out with a bang!" My last Sunday there, it was my turn to teach the Relief Society lesson. My calling was RS president at the time. While I wasn't bold enough to bear my testimony of the falseness of the Church, I *did* give a lesson I entitled, "Beware of False Prophets." I told the ladies to rely on the Bible and said they shouldn't just believe everything that our leaders taught, but instead should test it to see if it's truth (quoting from 1 John 4:1). It's kind of funny, but the 1st Counselor in the bishopric sat in on the lesson that day. He thought it was so good that he asked if I would speak in Sacrament Meeting the following Sunday. I was almost tempted to stay one more week so I could have an opportunity to warn more people.

That afternoon I called the Bishop and asked him if he could drop by the house. When he did, I gave him my resignation letter and temple recommend and told him I was resigning from the Church (you can read the full story in my book *Mormonism, the Matrix and Me*).

It had already been almost a month since I came to the conclusion the Church wasn't true. During that time, I began listening to verse-by-verse Bible studies for a couple hours each day, and the things I learned were so exciting to me that I was eager to find a good church. I wanted to make up for lost time. I didn't let any time lapse between leaving Mormonism and embracing traditional Christianity. For the last several years I've studied the Bible from a Messianic Jewish perspective, which has deepened my love and appreciation for Jesus and helped me understand the gospel better; but when I first left Mormonism I found a lot of comfort and healing in a Southern Baptist church. It took me about three weeks—and visiting a half dozen different churches on Sundays and Wednesday evenings—before I found one that resonated with me.

Immediately, I got involved in a weekly women's Bible study. I found a mentor who taught me the differences between Mormonism and Christianity. We met every Tuesday afternoon for months, going through a non-denominational study guide that taught the basic tenets of the Christian faith. I joined an online support group called MIT-Talk, for Mormons in Transition, a group for those who "still believe Jesus has the answers, but [aren't] sure the Mormon Church does."

I wrote about my experience in discovering that Mormonism isn't true—sometimes called an "exit story"—and made a booklet out of it. I bought some brightly-colored paper for the cover, made copies at OfficeMax, and stapled them together to hand them out wherever I could. It was called *How the Other Woman Led me to Christ: a Relief Society President's Journey out of Mormonism.* It still circulates around the internet. Not everyone who leaves the Church will feel a need to be vocal about it or to spread the news, but for me it was therapeutic. I only wish I had been more tactful and sensitive.

Christians began asking me if I would come speak at their churches to share my testimony of leaving Mormonism and coming to faith in Christ. Every time I told my story publicly, I went through a catharsis that helped me break free of Mormonism. You'll find your own path to recovery. Do what works for you. It might be that you just want to walk away and never look back. Just because you're an ex-Mormon it doesn't mean you have to become an activist of some kind. It's not a requirement.

If you're not ready to get involved in another church or your present circumstances don't allow for it, take care of your spiritual needs by listening to sermons or teachings online. Read inspirational books. Get a good study Bible and immerse yourself in God's word. The psalms bring comfort and understanding; Proverbs gives instruction and counsel. After Dennis and Rauni Higley (H.I.S. Ministries International) left Mormonism, they and their three children listened to Bible study tapes (this was before the internet) every Sunday for three years before they felt ready to start attending a church!

If you need counseling, it's nothing to be ashamed of. Counseling can be especially helpful if you're having problems sleeping, experiencing a loss of appetite, suffering depression or anxiety, or just having trouble dealing with day to day activities. Furthermore, a good counselor can help you work through the strain put on your relationships caused by rejecting Mormonism.

Many ex-Mormons find it therapeutic to journal. Write down your feelings, your experiences, your anger, and your fears. This is for your eyes only. Putting your frustrations, failures, and successes, and discoveries in writing can be beneficial as you look back and see how you overcame your challenges.

Make sure you're eating right. Don't overload on sugar and high-carb foods. Take good quality fish oil, vitamin D3, and other supplements as directed by your doctor. Get fresh air. Exercise, even if it's just walking around the block or a shopping mall. Your health is important. When people go through times of stress they're apt to neglect their health. Lack of sleep, poor diet, and worry makes a person foggy-minded, on edge, and exhausted. Take good care of yourself.

This might seem simplistic, but surround yourself with uplifting music and motivational speeches (for example, *Ted Talks*, online). Read inspirational literature or blogs. This is not just putting a band-aid on a gaping wound; this is putting you a hopeful frame of mind so you can move forward.

Finally, start a new hobby or take up an old one. Maybe wine-making, eh? Join a club. Meet new people. Take some fun classes at your local college or Parks and Recreation Department. Learn to dance, paint, or do wood carving. Become a coffee snob! Get involved in positive, uplifting things. Do "random acts of kindness" (no, that term did not originate with the Mormons). People often feel better about themselves and life in general when they are engaged in helping others. Connect with people; it's important for your mental and emotional health.

7

Throwing Baby Jesus Out With the Bathwater

"When I began my career as a cosmologist some twenty years ago, I was a convinced atheist. I never in my wildest dreams imagined that one day I would be writing a book purporting to show that the central claims of Judeo-Christian theology are in fact true, that these claims are straightforward deductions of the laws of physics as we now understand them. I have been forced into these conclusions by the inexorable logic of my own special branch of physics."

"From the perspective of the latest physical theories, Christianity is not a mere religion, but an experimentally testable science."

~ Frank Tipler, Professor of Mathematical Physics and co-founder of the anthropic principle

What has been the hardest part about leaving the Church?

I don't know how to separate fact from fiction. My realty is based on a lie I lived for 61 years, so consequently I just find it easier to not believe anything.

Fear! The programming that all churches were wrong made me feel that I had no where to go. Being shunned by friends and family.

Weak understanding of the biblical Jesus or the Bible.

Feeling like I had been ripped out of my life-long comfort zone and dropped in an unfamiliar place with no map or rules. I didn't know what values I had or what should be important to me.

No longer feeling confident in having a "sure knowledge" of how everything will play out in the afterlife.

Feeling confused. Cast adrift without any sense of what was real or right.

One of the biggest adjustments after leaving the Church is navigating the turbulent waters of uncertainty. For many, we don't just lose a community, we lose a whole faith. We lose a way of life. Our worldview that we were once so sure of, is shaken to the core. It's like being dropped into the ocean and told to swim to shore. The problem is that we can't see land anywhere! We feel like we were blind-folded and tagged "It" in a cosmic game of Marco Polo; we can hear distant voices calling out to us, but have no bearing on which way to go. What is real? As one of the survey responders stated, it seems easier to just not believe anything.

It's hard to get an actual percentage because of lack of polling data, but from my experience in the ex-Mormon community, the majority of people who leave Mormonism become agnostic, atheist, or consider themselves "spiritual" rather than religious. The term "religious" has become somewhat negative in our culture, but being religious isn't necessarily a bad thing. It simply means "believing in or relating to a religion." The question ex-Mormons ask themselves is if any religion is true. Given the pain associated with discovering that Mormonism is false, and furthermore that it has been promulgated by its leaders through deception, it's no wonder individuals leaving the Church turn their backs on religion altogether! In reality though, it isn't fair or wise to lump all religions into the same category, just as it we can't generalize that all men, or all women, all _____ (insert ethnic group), all pharmaceuticals, all movies, or all what-have-you are bad.

For instance, if you've had bad experiences with Ford motor vehicles all your life are you going to give up driving and just walk or skateboard everywhere from now on or are you going to do some research and find a car manufacturer that puts out quality vehicles? If you discovered that the poison ivy you've been dicing up and adding to your salads isn't actually a type of vegetable, and in fact is what has been making you sick for the last 10 years, are you going to give up on eating real vegetables and become a carnivore? No! You're going to get educated on wild plants and learn what is nutritional and what is poison. The misfortune that a dishonest salesman sold you a fake Gucci handbag or a knockoff Rolex doesn't negate the fact that genuine Gucci and Rolex products exist. So you've been had, duped, suckered, and perhaps with devastating consequences. It doesn't mean that there is no "Real Deal." After all, what is an imitation? It's something that appears on the surface to be the genuine article, but it's a counterfeit; a copy of something real.

Leaving Mormonism is a difficult process to go through. You're shocked, angered, saddened, confused, and mentally and emotionally exhausted. Additionally, you're at your most vulnerable. The last thing you want is to be deceived again.

As I was in the process of discovering that Mormonism wasn't true, there were a few days when I wondered if God was even real and if there actually were truths about him that could be discovered. I relived a moment from childhood during those few days. I was reminded of when I learned that Santa Claus wasn't real at the age of eight. For some kids it's no big deal, but for me it was devastating. I adored my mother and hung on her every word, believing and having solid faith in everything she said. When the boy next door told me that Santa wasn't real, that it was just parents putting presents under the Christmas tree, I didn't believe him. I told him that wasn't true . My mother told me he was real and she never lied. Immediately I marched back home and went to my mom.

"Guess what Brian told me! He said that Santa isn't real and that it's just you putting the presents under the tree! I told him he was wrong." I stood there resolutely, indignant at the gall Brian had to besmirch my mother and say something so ridiculous. I knew Santa was real! First, that's what I was told all my life. Second, there were dozens of cartoons on television between Thanksgiving and Christmas that all revolved around Santa. Charlie Brown believed in Santa. Rudolph believed in Santa. And third, the milk and cookies I set out on Christmas Eve were always gone Christmas morning. Clearly that was all evidence that Santa Claus was indeed real.

My mother's face clouded as she made some comment about the "little brat next door" having to spoil everything. Instead of coming to my defense and vindicating me, she said, "Well, you're going to find out sooner or later anyway. Santa is just pretend."

I stared at her, stunned and incredulous. My lower lip began to quiver and I burst into tears. "You, you lied to me." She insisted she didn't lie; it was just pretending for fun. I asked with trepidation, "What about the Easter Bunny and the Tooth Fairy?"

"Same as Santa," she said. "Just pretend."

"Is God real?" Fear suddenly grasped me.

"Of course he's real. Don't be silly."

"How do I know you're not lying about that too?"

My normally sweet mother got angry and said, "Oh stop it! Stop being a baby," and with that, she walked out of the room leaving me to come to grips with reality on my own.

The experience stuck with me, and when I had children of my own I told them that Santa Claus was just for fun. When they asked me why other parents told their kids Santa was real and how come I didn't, I explained that I wanted them to be able to trust me and didn't ever want them to wonder if I was telling them the truth about God. Ironically, my kids became the "brats next door" that spoiled Christmas for all the neighborhood kids. My bad.

Also ironic, now that I think about it, was that I hadn't been telling them the truth about God as they grew up; unintentionally of course, but falsehood nonetheless. I taught them that God was once a human like us, who grew up on a world in a galaxy far, far away. He became righteous during his lifetime; so righteous that he was able to advance to godhood and create worlds of his own, like all the gods before him did. I taught them we had a Heavenly Mother (probably more than one), and that someday we could become like them and have spirit children and create our own worlds for them to be born on. I was perpetuating Joseph Smith's myth, a fairytale that I mistook for fact. And my children trusted me. It was only natural for them to feel confused and betrayed when I left the Church and told them I had been wrong about it being true.

Suddenly, I was again confronted with the same feelings of confusion and fear that I had as a child. Is God real? Is there truth outside of Mormonism? How can I trust my judgment going forward? If I couldn't even discern the errors of Mormonism, how would I ever be able to discern anything? How could I learn to separate fact from fiction? I had to go back to square one: Is there a God?

It would be easier if God just wrote in big cloudy letters across the sky: I AM GOD! I CREATED THE UNIVERSE! But how could we prove it was God doing it and not a small fleet of airplanes releasing smoke to form sentences? I suppose if there were airplanes skywriting instead of the finger of God we would see them; but still, there would always be a reason for people to be skeptical. No, even seeing a huge finger appear in the sky would do nothing to "prove" conclusively that God exists. That might have been compelling anciently or as late as 100 years ago; however, with all the astounding technology we currently have, a phenomenon like that could be written off as sleight of hand, illusion, or special effects of some sort.

We all bring our own set of biases to the table through which we interpret the world and new information. This is why as individuals we can believe or not believe something despite evidence to the contrary. That's why signs and wonders will not convince someone who doesn't want to be convinced.

In a much more powerful way than writing cloud sentences, God has revealed himself through the things he created:

> Because what is known about God is plain to them, since God has made it plain to them. For ever since the creation of the universe his invisible qualities—both his eternal power and his divine nature—have been clearly seen, because they can be understood from what he has made. (Romans 1:19-20)

When I thought about how diverse, magnificent, and intricate every aspect of life is, from the ecosystem to anatomy and physiology to geology and astronomy and everything in between, there is just no way this all happened by chance or evolution. It isn't rational, from my perspective, to accept that everything just sort of evolved over time. It defies the

2nd law of thermodynamics (entropy), which states that there is a natural tendency to go from order to disorder; not the other way around.

> *If it is only for this life that we have put our hope in the Messiah, we are more pitiable than anyone.*
> *(1 Corinthians 15:19)*

I know that the theory of the Big Bang, without God as the original cause, is more complex than this, but in its most basic form it seems to defy logic: First there was nothing, and then it exploded and became everything, and continued to get better over time. That doesn't seem reasonable to me. I may as well believe in Santa Claus and that he can visit every single home on Planet Earth and deliver toys all in one night.

For me, knowing that God exists is more than an intellectual exercise alone. From childhood onward I've had personal experiences with what is often termed "the supernatural." Millions of people have experienced or witnessed inexplicable things, whether it be miraculous healings, demonic manifestations, premonitions of danger, and other phenomena outside the realm of our physical dimension. Some of it can be explained away, but not all.

I reaffirmed my prior conclusion that God does indeed exist. I don't have enough faith to be an atheist. Once that was settled in my mind, I had to find out if Jesus was really the Messiah, and did he, in fact, rise from the dead, for; "If it is only for this life that we have put our hope in the Messiah, we are more pitiable than anyone" (1 Corinthians 15:19).

I went on a research feeding frenzy! A flurry of books, lectures, symposiums—I was reading and listening until all hours of the night. It was mentally and emotionally exhausting, and yet, through it all I felt a comforting peace, freedom, and joy that I had never experienced to that extent before. I was excited and amazed by all the actual evidence that the Bible was reliable, that Jesus was a real historical figure, and that there is compelling evidence for his resurrection.

The Biblical Faith is not Like Mormonism

Mormonism was birthed in the fertile imagination of Joseph Smith. There is no archaeological evidence for the Book of Mormon. No written record exists because the "Angel Moroni" conveniently (or inconveniently) took the Gold Plates back from Smith and hid them once again in the Hill Cumorah. We see a pattern of changing stories, historical revisions, doctrinal inconsistencies and contradictions, and the claim that the only way to test the veracity of Mormonism is through faith and a spiritual witness (feelings) alone.

In Mormonism, investigators and members must rely on hearsay evidence, whether it comes from early leaders of the Church and the testimonies of the eleven witnesses to the Book of Mormon or from members standing up in Fast & Testimony Meetings to tell the congregation that they "know the Church is true." The mantra of Mormonism is "Follow the Brethren;" don't question, don't think too much, and don't go outside of what the prescribed manuals and guidelines direct.

Conversely, Biblical faith is based on the Bible, a collection of 66 books, penned by over 40 writers, over the course of thousands of years. An abundance of archaeological and historical evidence exists, demonstrating that the people, places, and events in the biblical record were real. Manuscripts have been tested over time and found to be consistent. One of the most remarkable discoveries was the complete book of Isaiah, found among many other ancient texts at Qumran. It was 1,000 years older than the oldest manuscript available at the time, and with only a few minor spelling variations it was unchanged.

Is there proof for every person and event mentioned in the Bible? No, but if the authenticity of the things we have evidence for can be tested and verified, then we can have confidence that the Bible is trustworthy in the areas that we do not yet have evidence for.

No one says, "Pray about the Bible and ask God to show you if it isn't true." Judeo Christianity is not comprised of blind faith, nor is it based on intellectual exercise alone. It combines knowledge (examination of the facts) and belief (trust, faith). As Messianic Jewish author and translator David H. Stern wrote;

> The head has its way of knowing, and the heart has its way of knowing, and neither should be ignored. If head and heart are connected, there is the possibility that what the Bible claims, seems and proves to be will move the heart to respond in faith. If one believes that in the Bible God is speaking, one will be much more likely to take seriously its promises, threats, suggestions and commands; and the result, I propose, will be a better life for oneself and the others one meets (Complete Jewish Bible, 1998, p. xxvii).

In addition to archaeological evidence (artifacts) and historical documents outside the Bible that corroborate its accounts, fulfilled prophecies support the reliability of the Bible. There are many specific prophecies dated before the actual events occurred, regarding people, places, and things that later happened exactly as prophesied.

The limited size and scope of this chapter precludes going into detail about the biblical record and compelling evidence for the resurrection of Jesus Christ. Tomes have been written on the subject by people much more qualified than I. *My* purpose is to encourage and persuade you to hold on to your faith; don't throw baby Jesus out with the bathwater. Just because the Mormon Church isn't true, doesn't mean that God isn't real or Jesus doesn't matter or that there isn't a special purpose for your life.

Think of it like this: Mormonism is like counterfeit money. Undetected, counterfeit money can do good things: buy food and clothing, pay bills, purchase gifts, get your car fixed (or your teeth); however, when it gets to the bank—where it really counts—it won't pass inspection. The individuals making the bills are guilty of a crime and at some point will be dealt with by the proper authorities. Meanwhile, does the fact that there is counterfeit money circulating keep you from working, earning, saving, and spending? Of course not. Why? Because you know that the existence of counterfeits (money, knock-off Rolex watches, imitation Gucci bags) does not vitiate the genuine articles.

Similarly, the existence of false religions, cults, aberrant teachings, deceptive ideologies, business scams, fake news, and falsehoods of all kinds does not eliminate truth where it exists. Don't let a counterfeit keep you from being connected to a vibrant, loving Christian community. Spiritual truth is not found in one specific denomination. Salvation is not dependent upon your membership in the right church or club. God's mercy, love, and grace isn't only available to certain classes of people or limited to card-carrying members of a particular organization. Access to God isn't based on how much tithing we give or how "worthy" we are or how frequently we attend church or synagogue.

Truth isn't found in a location; it's found in a Person. Jesus is the Way, the Truth, and the Life. Don't close your mind and heart because of the pain of finding out you had been deceived by the Mormon Church. And remember, people aren't perfect. There are hypocrites in every religion and "non-religion." Who, of any of us, ever truly lives up to the standards we set for ourselves or claim to believe in? We all fall short; every single one of us. The God of Abraham, Isaac, and Jacob is perfect: people aren't. You may have been hurt by individuals, but God will never leave you or forsake you. As you go through the trials and challenges of life he is there to sustain you and direct your paths.

8

Dealing with Toxic People

"Toxic people defy logic. Some are blissfully unaware of the negative impact that they have on those around them, and others seem to derive satisfaction from creating chaos and pushing other people's buttons."

~ Dr. Travis Bradberry, author of Emotional Intelligence 2.0

If you're able to walk away from the LDS Church with the support of family and friends, count yourself among the lucky ones. Most individuals leaving the Church get pushback of some kind from Mormon relatives and acquaintances. While you can expect resistance, negative reactions, heated arguments, awkward conversations, and strained relationships, what should you do when things turn toxic? What is the difference between the natural disappointment or alarm exhibited by loved ones when they care about you and are afraid for your eternal welfare and harmful overreactions? What behavior is reasonable and acceptable? What kind of responses are unacceptable? Does "turning the other cheek" mean passively letting someone walk all over you or hurt you over and over?

When you exit Mormonism it's reasonable to expect that your active LDS spouse, parents, or children are going to be upset. Angry words might be exchanged. Hurtful comments might be made. But in healthy relationships where there is mutual respect and genuine love, people reconcile. Apologies are made. Understanding and conflict resolution are pursued. The road may be rocky for a while, but ultimately trust is restored and fellowship returns.

Conversely, toxic people are akin to emotional vampires who suck you dry and leave you drained of life and vitality. The following are examples of people who might qualify as toxic:

- The sister who refuses to let you see her children any more.
- The sister-in-law who returns all your Christmas and birthday cards unopened.
- The parents or in-laws who try to get custody of your children.
- The brother who calls you every few days to tell you that you're going to hell or "Outer Darkness."
- The Bishop who keeps telling you that you are responsible for destroying your family.
- The co-worker or neighbor who spreads gossip about you.
- A spouse (or ex-spouse) who tries to turn your children against you.
- Ward members that tell your children negative or untrue things about you or why you left the Church.
- A church leader who encourages your spouse to divorce you.
- Children or teens who bully your kids at school because you or your family left the Church.

Toxic people are those who cannot allow you to leave their presence with your dignity intact. They are controlling, manipulative, and punitive. They try to shame you for your decision to leave the Church and blame you for all the family's ills or misfortunes. They're successful at making you wonder if *you're* the crazy one.

As followers of Christ, how do we demonstrate the love of God while protecting ourselves or our families from emotional abuse? In the book *Boundaries* (which I highly recommend buying and keeping on hand for reference), authors Henry Cloud and John Townsend advocate setting limits on one's exposure to destructive people and relationships. On setting up limits;

> In reality, setting limits on others is a misnomer. We can't do that. What we can do is set limits on our exposure to people who are behaving poorly; we can't change them or make them behave right.
>
> Our model is God. He does not really "set limits" on people to "make them" behave. God sets standards, but he lets people be who they are and then separates himself from them when they misbehave, by saying in effect, "You can be that way if you choose, but you cannot come into my house." Heaven is a place for the repentant, and all are welcome.
>
> But God limits his exposure to evil, unrepentant people, as should we. Scripture is full of admonitions to separate ourselves from people who act in destructive ways (Matt. 18:15-17; 1 Cor. 5:9-13). We are not being unloving. Separating ourselves protects love, because we are taking a stand against things that destroy love (pp. 45-46).

It comes down to what we learned in kindergarten; if you can't say something nice, don't say anything at all, only taking it one step further by insisting, "If you can't say something in a respectful, calm, or kind way, then I choose not to listen to you." Other responses you might give;

"If you continue to verbally abuse me, I'll end the phone call.

"As long as we can stick to the issues and have respectful conversation, you're welcome in my home. Otherwise I'll ask you to leave."

"If you continue to speak badly about me to my children, you'll be restricted from seeing them."

"As soon as you're calm we can continue this discussion."

"I don't feel comfortable around you when you're raising your voice."

"You can continue yelling if you want to, but I will leave the room."

The fact is you cannot control other people or how they choose to behave, but you *can* control how you respond and whether or not you will accept their negative or hurtful treatment of you. We train people how to treat us by what we choose to tolerate from them. If we continually take verbal abuse from someone without flinching or removing ourselves from their presence, we are in essence teaching them that we do not value ourselves or the relationship. Setting boundaries for yourself is a way of guarding your heart, not only from pain inflicted by others, but from becoming cold and hardened.

We were created for companionship with God and fellowman. But when we're in a toxic relationship with one or more people (or separating from an unhealthy group or spiritually abusive system) the temptation is to cut ourselves off from everyone and refrain from forming new relationships that could be healthy and rewarding. Sometimes on the rebound we jump into relationships with a different set of people who may not have our best interests at heart. We're likely to come across ex-Mormons (or ex-whatever-religion) who haven't yet recovered and are still stuck in the bitter or resentful stage many years after their departure from Mormonism. They may try to encourage us to turn our backs on God, family, marriage, or the values we once stood for at the most vulnerable time of our lives. The best thing we can do for ourselves is to take time to evaluate our personal situations and make careful decisions with as much wisdom, planning, and forethought as possible.

There will be those who use guilt to try to manipulate or control you. My bishop tried to use this tactic on me. After repeated attempts over several months to have my name removed from the records of the Church, with the bishop stonewalling all along the way, I finally let him know I would take legal action if he did not process my request (side note: it is no longer necessary to go through your bishop to have your name removed). His immediate response was, "How could you do this after all I've done for you and your family?"

Other examples of guilting or shaming include:

How could you do this to your family?

If you're really a "Christian" now, you wouldn't be so [fill in the blank].

After all the Church has done for you, you turn your back on it!

If you cared about your family you wouldn't be doing this.

If you really loved me you would stop thinking about yourself for a change!

You never had a real testimony to begin with.

I can't believe you would hurt your parents like this. You're making the family look bad.

Keep in mind that just because a friend or loved one says something like one of the above examples doesn't make the person toxic. You have to look at their overall pattern of behavior. A toxic person almost always uses his or her anger or negativity to control others. If you can learn not to react to their attempts, then you are learning not to be controlled by them. You can respond in a loving or concerned way without giving in to manipulation:

I see how upset you are. You must be scared about my decision to leave the Church.

I appreciate all you've done for me; but this isn't about you.

Whether I had a testimony in the past or not, my decision to leave the Church is based on present evidence.

I'm sorry that my parents feel hurt, but they always taught me to choose the right, and I'm choosing the right by leaving.

This isn't about making the family look good or bad; it's about personal integrity and honesty.

Later in my conversation with the bishop, he said, "I can't believe you would do this to your family."

I replied, "If *you* came to the conclusion the Church isn't true, you would do the same thing."

As we talked, he tried to get me to promise not to go public or write a book. I told him I couldn't make that promise. He said something like, "Look, if you don't believe the Church is true, why don't you just quietly move on? Why try to destroy other people's faith?"

"Bishop," I said, "if you really believed that the Church was deceiving people and leading them away from the true God, you would want to warn them too."

In every instance I was able to respond without arguing or allowing myself to be shamed into changing my mind. He had no response to my rejoinders other than to shake his head in sadness. I was understanding and kind, but resolute. I set my boundaries by not accepting the guilt and shame the bishop tried to lay upon me.

It can be difficult at times to set boundaries because we care about our loved ones. We don't want to hurt or upset them. We don't want them to be angry or disappointed with us. We hate conflict. We fear rejection. Setting limits on our exposure to destructive behavior is risky because we may indeed experience rejection or conflict or make someone angry; however, to stay in those situations is ultimately harmful to all parties involved. It enables the other person to continue being verbally abusive or using inappropriate methods to communicate their feelings, and it takes a toll on our own emotional health and well-being. People who are always angry have a character flaw, unmet needs, or unresolved emotional pain from something in their past; and until they acknowledge and address it they'll continue hurting other people and being miserable themselves. Sometimes it takes others refusing to accept their anger before they decide to deal with it or get help.

On the other side of the coin, it's important to respect the boundaries that others have set. You might be in a family where someone has cut you off, even though you've only shown love and kindness. A few relatives or friends might be so angry and hurt over you leaving the Church that they block your texts, "unfriend" you on social media, or tell you that you're no longer welcome in their homes. They might forbid you to contact them or their children. And to be frank, there really isn't a lot you can do about that other than to respect their wishes and pray for them. It's a spiritual battle, after all.

NOTE: In this chapter I'm specifically addressing anger and manipulation as it applies to leaving Mormonism, although the basic principles can apply in other circumstances as well. If you are in a physically abusive relationship, separate yourself immediately from that situation and get help!

If you're trapped in a polygamy group, there is help available to arrange for your escape and provision. "*A Shield and a Refuge*" (shieldandrefuge.org) is a fantastic and trustworthy organization that can help women who want to leave Fundamentalist Latter-day Saint groups (FLDS).

Reference:

http://www.talentsmart.com/articles/How-Emotionally-Intelligent-People-Handle-Toxic-People-1028629190-p-1.html

9

Conclusion

"Rejoice in your hope, be patient in your troubles, and continue steadfastly in prayer. Share what you have with God's people, and practice hospitality. Bless those who persecute you—bless them, don't curse them! Rejoice with those who rejoice, and weep with those who weep. Be sensitive to each other's needs—don't think yourselves better than others, but make humble people your friends. Don't be conceited. Repay no one evil for evil, but try to do what everyone regards as good. If possible, and to the extent that it depends on you, live in peace with all people."

~ Romans 12:12-18

We've looked at the five most common mistakes individuals make as they leave the LDS Church:

- Being tactless and insensitive
- Forcing our new views on our LDS family and friends
- Going to extremes ("rebellious" or "adolescent" phase)

- Living in fear and regret
- Isolation, neglecting our needs

I confess I've made the first four. Let's transform these destructive actions into constructive ones.

Using Tact and Sensitivity

"More information is always better than less. When people know the reason things are happening, even if it's bad news, they can adjust their expectations and react accordingly. Keeping people in the dark only serves to stir negative emotions." ~ Simon Sinek

If you're married, your spouse deserves to know where you stand. Find a time when you can talk uninterrupted and aren't limited by a deadline. Whether you've had doubts about the Church for a long time or everything happened fast and unexpected, say so.

When I first began researching Mormon Church history, it wasn't because I was looking for ways or excuses to not believe in it any more. I was looking because I wanted to bring my friend who had "apostatized" back into the Church. I wanted to prove she was wrong. Instead, I found the opposite; she was right. So, when I told my family of my decision, I made sure they knew I wasn't looking for reasons to leave.

Regardless of how you came about discovering that Mormonism isn't what it claims to be, the most important thing you can do up front is to express your love and commitment to your spouse and that your feelings about the Church are not at all a rejection of him or her, nor a dismissal of morality. This is a big issue because many faithful LDS believe that to leave the Church means throwing out one's morals to live a life of debauchery. Reassure your spouse by saying what you do believe:

> I still believe in God. I believe in Jesus. I believe in morality and doing good. I believe in the sanctity of marriage. I want to love you and honor you with all my heart, and even in ways that maybe I haven't before. I want to "take things to a new level." I want us to be godly parents who teach our kids to live with integrity and good character. My feelings about the Church haven't diminished my commitment to the family one tiny bit. In fact, I feel a greater sense of love and responsibility in my calling as a [husband, wife].

Naturally, you'll need to modify that for the way you personally speak and feel. As might be expected, there is going to be a lot of fear on your spouse's part and a need for reassurance. Granted, there's fear on your part as well because you don't know how your spouse will react. Or maybe you know exactly what the reaction will be and that's what worries you! It isn't necessary to figure out all the answers during your first discussion together. Your spouse might need some time to let the news soak in. Ask your husband or wife to keep this between the two of you for at least a few days.

Understand that the news of your "loss of testimony" might be as much of a shock to your spouse as it was for you to discover the Church isn't true. The tendency for ex-Mormons is to immediately begin pummeling TBM family members with a barrage of anti-Mormonism materials, lengthy speeches, and frequent tirades against the Church and its leaders. However, it will be more effective to shower them with greater love, more patience, extra kindness and understanding, and using actions and good deeds rather than words to win them over to the real Messiah, Jesus.

I cannot overemphasize the importance of checking our hearts and examining ourselves to make sure our motivation is right. If we are more concerned with showing them how wrong Mormonism is than demonstrating through actions how right the love of the Living God is, we will actually be hindering them from receiving the truth.

How long were you or I faithful Mormons before being brought out? For me it was 26 years. Looking back over my life I can see how God prepared my heart to receive the truth. It was a slow process. Yes, there is an urgency to proclaim the gospel because we never know when it will be someone's last day on earth, including our own. But I think we can get so anxious about bringing our loved ones out of Mormonism that we put ourselves in the role of redeemer. You and I can't "save" anybody. Salvation is a work of God alone. We can deliver the gospel message, but ultimately it is the Holy Spirit who convicts someone of sin and opens the eyes of the spiritually blind.

We raised chickens for a time when I was a kid, and I learned something interesting. If you try to help a baby chick hatch by pulling the shell off, it will die. Why? In short, because it can take up to 24 hours after the chick pecks its first hole through the eggshell (pipping) before it continues pecking around the circumference (zipping). During the time the chick is in the process of hatching, it has to absorb the yolk sac, as well as prepare its lungs to breathe the outside air. A lot is going on *in* the shell before the chick is able to sustain life on the outside. So when you feel sorry for the little chick and try to "help" it come out of the shell you're actually contributing to its demise.

Trying to get family members out of Mormonism through tugging, pushing, and pulling (like tearing the shell off a chick) is going to result in *aversion* rather than *conversion*. You cannot force someone to believe something against their will. They will dig in their heels if they feel like their beliefs are being attacked.

Give Your Spouse and Teenagers Permission to Keep Believing

What I mean by this is to recognize that your family isn't going to stop believing in Mormonism just because you did. When a person's paradigm is threatened, he or she may cling tighter to their beliefs. If you want your husband, wife, or teens to be open to new ideas and new information, they have to feel like you're not trying to prove them wrong. As the saying goes; "A man convinced against his will, is of the same opinion still."

A man convinced against his will, is of the same opinion still.

Allow your loved ones time to come to their own conclusions about the Church by providing them with information *when (and if) they ask for it*. Don't leave so-called anti-Mormon material lying around. Be respectful, just as you would want the same respect from them.

Lay some ground rules to avoid fruitless arguments. Say that you're willing to talk about the evidence, the facts, and the issues, but as soon as personal attacks and accusations arise, the conversation ends. Of course this goes both ways. Don't return insult for insult. It's unproductive and hurtful for two people—who are supposed to love and honor one another—to be engaged in verbal warfare and character assassination. For example;

"You just don't want to come to the ward anymore because you'd rather stay home and watch football. Any old excuse!"

"Well if all those stupid Sacrament talks weren't so boring, maybe I wouldn't want to stay home to watch football."

"You're just an apostate now; a sad, sorry apostate!"

"Better an apostate than a Mo-bot."

Can you see how quickly these kinds of conversations turn into ugly, hurtful exchanges that damage relationships? Practice better responses, especially if communication skills aren't your strong suit.

Here's a better way to handle the forgoing conversation;

> "You just don't want to come to the ward anymore because you'd rather stay home and watch football. Any old excuse!"
>
> "I understand how upset you must feel when I don't go to church with you. I'm not staying home to hurt you. I'm sorry for causing you pain."
>
> "Well, I just feel like I'm married to an apostate now. I feel like we don't have anything in common anymore!"
>
> "I know how upsetting this all is. I'd feel the same way if I were in your shoes. But honey, we still have a lot in common. We share our lives, our marriage, great kids, a home...I love you and I'm committed to you. We'll work through this together. I wouldn't want you to be late to the meetings. Can I drive you?"
>
> "Sweetie, I'm sorry I called you an apostate."
>
> "No worries."

Set rules for family discussions and allow one another to express their views without criticizing them. When your loved ones feel safe, listened to, and understood, it creates an environment conducive to exploring new or uncomfortable information. Continually trying to point out the errors of Mormonism will only serve to drive them deeper into it. It's better to win them over by your love and kindness and by your willingness to allow them time to process the difficult truths they've been presented with.

Maintaining Morality

When I made the official announcement to my children that I no longer believed in Mormonism and was leaving the Church, my 15-year-old daughter burst into tears because she was afraid I was going to become a drunken, cigarette-smoking lush or worse. Well, I wasn't interested in smoking; I valued my lungs too much. I had no desire to be a "hooker," but sure got perverse pleasure out of dressing like one. I'm sort of joking. However, I certainly went from long skirts and modest shirts to wearing fairly skimpy clothing. As far as drinking, I made no apologies for having a margarita at a Mexican restaurant or adding a shot of brandy to my tea (ostensibly to help me feel better when I had a cold).

When you change your lifestyle almost overnight, it reinforces a Mormon's beliefs that, A) the Church is true, and B) You left the Church because the standards were too hard for you to keep.

You've kept the Word of Wisdom probably all your life, so what's waiting a little while longer or being discreet? Not secretive, but discreet. It goes back to respect. If there's never been alcohol allowed in the house, it's probably not a good idea to bring it into your home now if it upsets your spouse, especially if you have children. It's hard on kids to get conflicting messages. There is plenty of time to introduce lifestyle changes slowly and respectfully.

As far as dressing modestly, it's unlikely that an ex-Mormon man is going to be prancing around the yard in a thong or mowing the lawn wearing nothing but a smile (and a Speedo) (well, on second thought, he might). If you're female leaving the Church, you can have fun buying new clothes while maintaining a modicum of modesty. Since I discovered Victoria's Secret (I'm not sure what her secret is, but I think it's that she wears red polka dot undies with a matching lace bra) it's like "Katie bar the door!" Hide the charge card because I'm about to rack up some "Angel points" (a reward program that earns you discounts). If your husband is still TBM, he might secretly enjoy seeing you in sexy underclothes instead of drab temple garments. Show him what it's like to be a Victoria's Angel. Maybe he won't feel so bad that you left the Church. I'm just playin'.

You can wear cute, fun clothes, especially in the summer, but it's not a good idea to show up to a ward activity in a miniskirt and fishnet stockings. Like I did. We went to the ward for my son's missionary farewell. After Sacrament meeting, when everyone had gone to their classes, I sauntered past the priesthood room as if I were a brunette Marilyn Monroe (the door was closed, thank goodness), threw my head back, put a hand on my hip and crooned, "Hey boys; want to practice a little polygamy?" The only one who saw me was my teenage daughter, who by then had also left Mormonism. We both giggled and left. That was the first time (and last time for many years) I went to Sacrament Meeting as an ex-Mormon.

That's awful now that I think about it. Not sashaying past the high priest group, but dressing like Brittany Spears for a missionary farewell. I'm surprised the bishop allowed me to sing the special musical number dressed like that (of course, he got to sit behind me on the stand...). Seeing me dressed like a hooker probably strengthened everyone's testimonies of the Church that day. All I can say is, don't try that in your own ward.

If you find yourself having to attend a ward event or meeting long after you've left the Church, you can wear something tasteful and classy while still being true to yourself. Remember, you are there as an ambassador of the true Christ. Let people see by your appearance, countenance, and attitude that you belong to the Living God!

Living with Hope and Trust

Coming out of the Church is hard at first, but things gets better with time. It might take months or it might take years; but life is worthwhile and amazing and wonderful! You can live, and I mean *really live* and enjoy each moment, knowing you don't have to "measure up" to meet some man-made standard of worthiness.

I read an editorial in a St. George, Utah newspaper about non-Mormon residents feeling discriminated against and being treated like second-class citizens. An LDS businessman bragged to the reporter that in non-LDS churches confessionals are "totally voluntary," but in the Mormon Church adults confess every two years to be worthy of the temple.[1] What a sad, sad thing for the man to say, and he doesn't even realize it. It's actually an indictment against Mormonism. Mormons are required to confess at appointed times. If they don't confess to their Bishops and Stake Presidents, they aren't considered worthy to go to the temple.

Compare that to a biblical view, one that is understood by Judaism and Christianity. God wants our *voluntary* confession of sin, one that springs out of a broken heart and a contrite spirit. Consider the parable of the proud man and the sinner:

> Also, to some who were relying on their own righteousness and looking down on everyone else, he told this parable:
>
> "Two men went up to the Temple to pray, one a Parush (Pharisee) and the other a tax-collector. The Parush stood and prayed to himself, `O God! I thank you that I am not like the rest of humanity—greedy, dishonest, immoral, or like this tax-collector! I fast twice a week, I pay tithes on my entire income, . . .'
>
> But the tax-collector, standing far off, would not even raise his eyes toward heaven, but beat his breast and said, `God! Have mercy on me, sinner that I am!'
>
> I tell you, this man went down to his home right with God rather than the other. For everyone who exalts himself will be humbled, but everyone who humbles himself will be exalted." Luke 18:9-14

Truly, this parable speaks of the hope we have in the Messiah Jesus. His yoke is easy; his burden is light. No more striving and scratching our way through each day, wondering if we are good enough, worthy enough, or acceptable enough to merit God's favor. What joy and peace we can have in Yeshua outside of Mormonism!

We no longer have to live in fear and regret. This doesn't mean there won't be consequences to our leaving the Church. Some ex-Mormons go through divorce, rejection, custody battles, loss of business, are kicked out of their homes by parents, and other heartbreaking situations. However, if we just hold on to hope, trusting God to see us through, being gentle with ourselves instead of living in self-defeat, things can and do get better.

Fully Engaging in Life

Use your freedom to make a difference in the world around you. Be involved. Make new friends. Set aside time for yourself. Solitude is different from isolation. Solitude has a positive connotation of having quiet time to think, relax, or "feed the soul." During this time you can pray, journal, study the Bible, read uplifting literature, relax in a hot tub, or to engage in whatever you find peaceful and soothing. Listen to your favorite music. Take walks.

If your family is supportive (maybe you have non-LDS family or maybe you're still on good terms with your TBM family), spend time doing fun things together. Find common interests. If you used to have regular Family Home Evenings or family prayer, you can still keep meaningful traditions; just modify them in ways that everyone can relate to and enjoy.

In my situation, my older six children (ages 10 to 20) remained True Blue Mormons the first year after I left the Church. As the kids were growing up, we always had daily family scripture reading, prayer, and a hymn. After I left the Church I wanted to continue our traditions, only without the LDS aspects. We traded the Book of Mormon for the Bible. I usually did the praying (because I didn't want to feel like we were praying to a false god). We sang hymns from a Christian hymnal instead of the LDS hymnbook. In other words, we found things we could agree on and focused putting our energies into those activities. Even though we disagreed on theological issues, family love and unity continued to be extremely important to all of us. Occasionally we had rough moments, especially during the first year, but we were committed to each other.

Consider taking your kids on day trips or road trips. Visit your adult children or grand-children. If that's not possible under the circumstances, then connect with old friends. Go to Disneyland; it's the happiest place on earth. I'm not being flippant. My point is, don't stop living and giving. Take a break by having an adventure. Recovery means moving ahead.

Moving Forward with Faith

Finally, be open to God. Be willing to trust again. Develop the sense of wonder and awe that comes with trusting a God who loves you. Pursue a relationship with him. Head-knowledge alone will not sustain you through tough times. Overcome the fear of getting close to God. It isn't his "fault" you were deceived. He opened your eyes and led you out of Mormonism, did he not?

Yes, you say, *but why didn't he bring me out sooner? Why did I have to waste all those years living a lie?*

There is a time and season for everything; *everything*. First off, we are not puppets on a string. The Almighty does not micromanage every aspect of our lives. We make bad choices and we make good choices. Often we are on the receiving end of choices made by others. It's called free will. We experience heartache, hardship, and sorrow in this life, but "joy comes in the morning." This mortal life we struggle through is a blip in time compared to the immortality that lies before us in the eternities. Despite our suffering, we can have a foretaste of the joy that lasts forever, and it comes through a personal relationship with the Messiah, Jesus.

Think of it this way; you can have all kinds of knowledge about a celebrity (perhaps your teenage heart-throb). You read all the teen magazines and have posters plastering your walls. You know his or her birthday, favorite color, favorite foods, hobbies, and how he or she spends each day. You can rattle off all kinds of trivia about the person. Maybe you even joined a fan club. But if you never met them in person, never dated or courted, and don't talk regularly on the phone, is all that knowledge going to translate into a lasting and meaningful relationship? No. It's nothing more than wishful thinking, like when I had my heart set on marrying Donny Osmond.

So, how do you have a relationship with God? It starts with repentance (turning *from* sin, and turning *to* God). It's recognizing that you depend on him and that it's the righteousness and merit of Jesus that puts you in right-standing with God, not your own. Ask him for forgiveness. Then learn about him and do good—not because your good works earn you brownie points—but because doing good, making the world a better place, and letting your light shine is evidence of your faith. It lets a lost and dying world know that you belong to him; that you are a disciple of Rabbi Yeshua, a follower of Jesus Christ. Maintain your relationship by praying regularly and studying Scripture. Just like our meaningful earthly relationships, our relationship with God blossoms and thrives with time and attention.

Final Words

You've been through a lot. I can relate, and so can hundreds of thousands of others who have left Mormonism. You're not alone. Don't give up on yourself. Don't give up on the people you love. You have a purpose in life. There is a special place for you (no, not the Funny Farm). I'm serious. You are unique. You have value. You were created in the image of God. Determine to make a difference in the lives of others, and the life that changes the most will be your own.

1. Flynn, Michael. "Do Non-Mormons Face Discrimination in Southern Utah?" The Independent - A Voice for Utah. Web. 2 June 2016. (Publication date unknown)

Appendix A

How to Resign from the LDS Church

Resigning is as simple as writing a formal resignation letter. Your letter can be as brief or elaborate as you wish, but should include the following components:

- Name
- Birthdate
- Baptism date
- Address
- Ward and stake you reside in (if known)

Send your letter directly to LDS headquarters and they will forward copies of your resignation local Church leaders based on your current address. Include the last ward that you know had your records.

In your letter you should state that you have resigned your membership as of that date, and request your name be removed from the records of the Church. Example:

I, Emma Smith (use your own name), formally resign my membership in The Church of Jesus Christ of Latter-day Saints as of today, April 6, 20xx (fill in the proper date).

You may state you understand the that consequences of name removal include cancelation of all temple blessings and church ordinances. You may request that you want the 30-day rescission period waived, but whether or not that request is honored is up to the bishop and stake president.

The preceding is all that is required in the letter to have your name removed. Some people who resign their membership go to great lengths to explain all the reasons they no longer believe Mormonism is true in order to make an impact on leaders receiving the letter. Others just simply send a concise request.

Send your letter directly to:

Member and Statistical Records Department
50 E North Temple St, Room 1372
Salt Lake City, UT 84150-5310

Additionally, it's also good to give a copy to your local leaders. It's recommended you either hand-deliver the letter to your bishop and stake president or send a certified letter through the mail. Although unnecessary, having the letters notarized assures church leadership that it's actually you requesting your name to be removed, and not someone playing a practical joke.

Writing and sending your resignation letter is probably the most intimidating or difficult part of leaving the Church initially, as far as formalities go. Be aware that the LDS Church does not actually remove your name from their records, as the Church is secretive about their membership data. Most likely they just move your name from their list of "believing" members to a file for those who "apostatize." Regardless, sending a resignation letter is an important step in freeing yourself from Mormonism's hold, spiritually and psychologically. It will also put a halt to monthly visits from home teachers or visiting teachers.

An alternative and more streamlined process of getting your name off LDS records is now available through;

quitmormon.com

QuitMormon is a free service provided by Mark A. Naugle, an ex-Mormon immigration attorney in Utah. Sending your resignation letter through his website results in the Church processing your request in a matter of weeks, instead of possibly months.

Appendix B

Special Situations

Students enrolled at BYU or BYU Satellite Schools

Church policy will not allow you to continue in your degree study program if you officially resign your church membership. According to the current official Church Education System Honor Code, students lose their good Honor Code standing, as well as their ecclesiastical endorsement, if they have been excommunicated, disfellowshipped, or disaffiliate themselves from the Church (have their names removed from Church records).

Whether you feel that is unfair, discriminatory, or persecution, unfortunately doesn't matter as far as the Church is concerned. While BYU *does* accept non-LDS students, ex-LDS students present a problem. This is because you signed an agreement as a condition of admission to the school while you were an active member of the Church. When you leave with the Church you are essentially breaking the agreement you originally signed. There is very little recourse. I'm not aware of any former Mormons successfully being reinstated as students, and legally

BYU—as a private school—has the right to deny admission or terminate the enrollment of a student based on its policies.

Should you continue your studies as an "undercover apostate?" What if you're in your junior or senior year? Consider the options. Your enrollment status is dependent on your activity and good standing in the Church. Do you want to continue going to the ward or branch, fulfilling callings, partaking of the Sacrament, and lying during temple recommend interviews to finish your degree?

It's not always easy. Sometimes sacrifices must be made for the sake of truth and integrity. We either have to "play the game" by all the rules or be willing to accept the consequences. The Church can't "make" a person believe. I'm sure there are many BYU students, professors, and church members who don't believe Mormonism is true; but they remain students or continue to teach classes and continue attending their wards because they believe they and their families benefit from their affiliation with the Church.

If you don't believe the Church is true and you have come to biblical faith in the God of Abraham, Isaac, and Jacob, then the right thing to do is follow the Apostle Paul's instruction;

> We try not to put obstacles in anyone's path, so that no one can find fault with the work we do. On the contrary, we try to commend ourselves in every way as workers for God by continually enduring troubles, hardships, calamities, beatings, imprisonments, riots, overwork, lack of sleep and food. We commend ourselves by our purity, knowledge, patience and kindness; by the [Holy Spirit]; by genuineness of love and truthfulness of speech...
>
> Do not yoke yourselves together in a team with unbelievers.
>
> 2 Corinthians 6:3-7, 14

If we "live a lie" for the sake of appearances, convenience, or to avoid negative consequences, then we're not being genuine or truthful and we're putting obstacles in the paths of those whom we wish to bring to a redeeming knowledge of Jesus the Messiah. God will bring good out of bad circumstances for those who love him and belong to him (Romans 8:28). You might not see the good right away, and things certainly won't be easy just because you are now a Christian; but take comfort in knowing that God honors those who honor him.

LDS Employment

It's a bit trickier here. If you are working directly for the Church as a CES instructor or university professor, or are employed by the Church at their headquarters or on Temple Square, the same policies are in place as for BYU's Honor Code. Your condition of employment rests on your good standing in the Church and your agreement to abide by its standards. Even if you keep the same moral standards, but disaffiliate yourself from the Church, they have the legal right to terminate your employment. Remember, the LDS Church is a privately owned and run corporation.

For example, let's say you were employed by "Big Box Mobile", but stopped believing in the quality of their products and services and you no longer agreed with the company's vision and values. If you started badmouthing Big Box Mobile, blogging about their inferior products, and making public Facebook posts about how much you can't stand their customer service; and additionally you wear clothing that advertises the competition, they have a right to fire you. Likewise, the Church, as a business organization, can terminate your employment.

It's a different story altogether if you work for a non-church owned business. Your LDS supervisor cannot fire you just because you left Mormonism. An LDS business owner cannot legally fire you for resigning from the Church. There are laws in place to protect people from being discriminated against because of age, race, sex, religion, etc. Your boss might look for other reasons to get rid of you (so be on guard), but he or she cannot fire you just because you are no longer Mormon. If you feel that you're a victim of religious discrimination at your non-Corporate-Church-owned place of employment, then contact a discrimination attorney or the Equal Employment Opportunity Commission (www.eeoc.gov).

Appendix C

Going Public

Purpose

If you haven't noticed yet, there are tons of blogs, websites, and books by former Mormons. This doesn't mean there isn't room for yours too, should you choose to go public. When deciding on what venue to use for your exit story, views, or advice, think about your purpose. Is it to inform and educate? Is it to vent frustration? Do you intend to reach out to Mormons to bring them to biblical faith? Are you trying to inspire others or help them in some way? Or do you just want to have a "public journal" portraying life through the lenses of an ex-Mormon?

Goals

Do you want to write on a regular basis or put a one-time statement or profile online? How much time do you plan to spend on your blog or website? What kind of topics do you want to cover? How much money are you willing to spend (domain name, hosting, print or eBook publishing)? What audience do you want to reach? What social media goals do you have? Will you post daily or weekly? Do you want to receive feedback, even from critics?

Speaking

Maybe your desire is to speak at various churches, Bible study or youth groups about how you left Mormonism and came to faith in Jesus. What topics do you think would benefit your audience? You might want to delineate the differences between LDS doctrine and Biblical doctrine, or you may want to simply tell your story. Do you know any pastors who are open to inviting you to speak? Have you contacted any ex-Mormon support or meet-up groups where you could share your testimony?

Answering Critics

Be prepared for ugly, accusatory emails from upset LDS individuals who attack your character or mock your Christian beliefs. It's tempting to respond in kind, but resist the temptation. Try not to "read into" their comments meanings that may not be there. Seek understanding. Ask for clarification. Respond with kindness, remembering that you, too, were once in the dark and unwilling or unable to see the light. As God so patiently worked in our lives, let us patiently let our "light so shine before people, so that they may see the good things [we] do and praise [our] Father in heaven" (Matthew 5:16).

Appendix D

Recommended Resources

Websites

- 4Mormon.org
- AdamsRoadBand.com
- EquippingChristians.com
- ExMormonFiles.com
- HisMin.com
- MormonInfo.org
- Mit.Irr.org
- MRM.org
- SacredGroves.net/video.htm
- ShieldAndRefuge.org
- UTLM.org
- WivesofJosephSmith.org

Books

◊ *Mormonism, the Matrix, and Me* / Tracy Tennant
◊ *Unveiling Grace* / Lynn K. Wilder
◊ *Words That Hurt, Words That Heal* / Rabbi Joseph Tellushkin
◊ *Sitting at the Feet of Rabbi Jesus* / Ann Spangler and Lois Tverberg
◊ *Assumptions that Affect Our Lives* / Dr. Christian Overman
◊ *Seven Reasons Why You Can Trust the Bible* / Erwin W. Lutzer
◊ *Cold-Case Christianity* / J. Warner Wallace
◊ *God Behaving Badly* / David T. Lamb
◊ *Boundaries* / Dr. Henry Clud and Dr. John Townsend

About the Author

As an active member of the Church of Jesus Christ of Latter-day Saints for 26 years, Tracy Tennant held many positions, including: Young Married Adult Activities Leader, Primary Teacher, Nursery Assistant, Assistant Ward Librarian, Ward Bulletin Specialist, Cub Scout Den Leader, Ward Music Chairman, Visiting Teaching Supervisor, Relief Society Teacher, and Relief Society President, among others. Tracy was a frequent vocalist and speaker at special youth and adult firesides. She was serving as Relief Society President when she resigned her membership in the LDS Church in December of 2000.

Tracy has a Bachelor of Arts in communication studies; Associate of General Studies (emphasis in early childhood education); and a Certificate of Achievement in Practical Nursing.

Currently, Tracy writes, blogs, and speaks on motherhood, family, and adult ADHD, as well as shares her experience and knowledge of Mormonism and Biblical Christianity.

CONNECT WITH TRACY:

TracyTennant@outlook.com

Facebook.com/FromKolobToCalvary

and look for From Kolob to Calvary's Podcast in iTunes!

More from Tracy Tennant

AVAILABLE ONLINE WHEREVER BOOKS ARE SOLD

Right Track Publishing

CPSIA information can be obtained
at www.ICGtesting.com
Printed in the USA
BVHW080730110520
579273BV00010B/312